DINNER & DISCIPLESHIP

DEVELOPING DEVOTION DAY BY DAY

BY MEGAN ANN SCHEIBNER

WITH CHEF EMMA SMOCK

Character Health
101 Casablanca Ct.
Cary, NC 27519

ISBN 978-0-9849714-7-3

Contents

INTRODUCING CHEF EMMA SMOCK

Emma Smock began life as Emily Marion Scheibner. She is our third child and second daughter. From her youngest days, Emma loved to cook, experiment, and generally, make a huge mess in my kitchen! After graduation from high school, Emma went on to college where she earned a degree in Culinary Arts, (graduating as Valedictorian of her class) and a second degree in Business. She's one smart cookie!

As I began the revisions of the Recipe and Routine series, it just made sense to involve Emma in the process. Characterhealth.com is truly a family business, with our children involved in every aspect. Choosing Emma to select, develop, and record recipes was an easy decision. It lifted a burden from me, and this time she got to make a mess in her own kitchen! While my recipes are yummy and family friendly, (Emma calls them "Mommy" food) they aren't always nutritionally balanced. There I said it! Sometimes, I cook what tastes good, even if it's not good for you!

Because of Emma's training as a chef and her extensive knowledge of nutrition and meal planning, she provides a great balance to my offerings. Although I gave her incredible editorial freedom, (You're welcome, Emma) I did manage to keep in a couple favorites like Cheeseburger Soup, (Lunch and Literature) and Breakfast Pizza. (Rise and Shine) She held her nose, but allowed me some leeway. Honestly, we don't eat those foods everyday, so I don't feel guilty at all! And, to set the record straight... Cheese curls are really just air, so what's the big deal!

Our family is very healthy with no food allergies, so the recipes you will find use basic ingredients. Please, adapt as necessary to fit your own dietary needs. I did have one daughter who was required to be gluten-free for a time, so I feel your pain. Thankfully, there are more and more substitutionary items to replace the non-gluten free ingredients.

I know you'll enjoy these new revisions and Emma's awesome recipes! I couldn't be prouder of her and working together was a blast... Even when she nagged me about my food choices! Now that she's a mommy, (Thanks for bringing us Oliver, Emma!) perhaps she'll start to eat more like me. Somehow, I doubt it!

> *"I know you'll enjoy these new revisions and Emma's awesome recipes! I couldn't be prouder of her and working together was a blast..."*

DINNER AND DISCIPLESHIP: DEVELOPING DEVOTION DAY BY DAY

Why Dinner and Discipleship? It's a simple concept, really. Scripture makes it clear that we, the parents, are the chief disciple-makers in our children's lives. We are the instruments, chosen by God, and responsible to implant Biblical truth, water the seeds of faith, and lovingly help our children to uproot sinful desires and appetites as they make themselves known to us. It's a huge task, but one made harder by our busy lives and mobile society.

In order to spend the time necessary investing in our children's spiritual wellbeing, we must intentionally make the time. That's where the dinner hour comes in. There is no better time, in my opinion, than the dinner hour to turn our attention to God, His Word, and our children's spiritual needs. The precedent for this time investment is found in Deuteronomy 6:6-7.

"And these words, which I am commanding you today, shall be on your heart; and you shall teach them diligently to your sons and shall talk of them when you sit in your house and when you walk by the way and when you lie down and when you rise up."

Nope, nothing in there about the dinner hour, but in our home, that's the one consistent time that I can count on all of us being together. That's the time I know that with full stomachs and focused parental attention, my children will begin to open their hearts and share what's happening in their worlds. That's the time that I can slow myself down to focus on the eternal without the distraction of places to go and people to see!

The dinner table is the place I can diligently "talk about these things" before we rise up and go our separate ways.

Dinner and discipleship, coupled together, really do provide a powerful ministry. Not only does dinner provide a great time to teach the "hows" of living the Christian life, as we practice hospitality through sharing our meal with others, our children learn the practical skills necessary to put into action the head knowledge of discipleship. As we work hard to portray excellence in our dinner preparation and our discipleship relationships, we will be elevating Christ and building a family testimony of faith and faithfulness.

I don't know about you, but although I work hard to serve a healthy breakfast, and although lunch is an always-necessary meal, my best efforts go into our family dinners. If you are anything like me, you spend far more time searching magazines and cookbooks for interesting and delicious dinner recipes, than for breakfast and lunch recipes. Why is that? I believe that there is something special about the dinner hour. Dinner represents more than just nourishment and food to fill the belly. Dinner is the time that we join in fellowship with our family and friends around a common table. Dinner is the time we open our home to folks that need friendship and encouragement. Dinner is the time we share God's bounty with others. Dinner deserves our best efforts.

In the same way, discipling our children is the piece de resistance of our child training. Although a decent and orderly routine to their day is helpful, and life skills learned through our example and teaching are necessary, I hope that those achievements are not the final goal you have in mind for your children. Our children could learn everything we have to teach them in all of these areas and still be nothing more than good moral citizens. That is certainly not a high enough goal!

I believe God has much higher goals and aspirations for our children than simple morality and obedience. His desire for our children is the same as His desire for us. This desire is found in Mark 12:30-31, "And you shall love the Lord your God with **all** your heart, and with **all** your soul, and with **all** your mind, and with **all** your strength. The second is this, you shall love your neighbor as yourself." (Emphasis mine) God wants us to be faithful followers who love the unlovely, serve the needy, pray for the hurting, and seek to obey Him completely. Just as much as He passionately desires this for us, His passion for our children is the same. As we diligently seek to fulfill this command, only then can we echo the Apostle Paul in saying, "I exhort you therefore, be imitators of me." (I Corinthians 4:16) This is the essence of discipleship, following so closely after Christ that we can exhort our children to do the same.

Discipleship has become somewhat of a lost art in our modern culture. Discipleship isn't just completing a bible study, although bible study is part of discipleship. Discipleship isn't just spending time praying with another believer, although prayer is an essential element of discipleship. Prayer isn't just serving together, or worshiping together, or fellowshipping together, although all of those things are certainly included in discipleship. No, discipleship is the process of walking alongside another believer and growing together in relationship with the Lord. Discipleship requires accountability, vulnerability, transparency, commitment, and sometimes, a good kick in the rear. Discipleship isn't about working through a study, but rather, walking together through life. Discipleship is long-term and eternity focused, not short-lived and needs of the moment driven.

As believers, we are called to be disciple makers. We are called to pass on what we've been taught and to encourage those we teach to do the same. As parents, our first and primary disciples live right under our roofs. Our children are learning firsthand what it means to live the Christian life as they study with us, pray with us, serve with us, fellowship with us, and incorporate God's Word into their hearts and habits with us. They will either learn relationship, or religion, as they follow our example. Relationship with Christ will strengthen them to follow the Lord in faithfulness. Religion may make our family "look" right in the short term, but in the long run, religion cannot provide the faith foundation that we and our children need in order to stand firm in a shaky world. Our commitment to disciple making in our home will take the important "head knowledge" we teach and turn it into "heart knowledge" our families can apply.

How then can we accomplish this discipleship in our homes? Let's take a moment to look at the book of Deuteronomy, once again. Deuteronomy 6:6-7 walks us through the process of discipleship. "And these words which I am commanding you today, shall be on your heart;" (our part in personal obedience) "and you shall teach them diligently to your sons and shall talk of them when you sit in your house and when you walk by the way and when you lie down and when you rise up" (our part in training our children). Discipleship is a 24- hour a day, 7 day a week proposition. Not a job for the weak at heart, but what wonderful fruit is possible for the diligently discipling parent and the faithfully obedient child.

But what if you've never been on the receiving end of a discipling relationship? What if you don't know the first thing about developing a daily discipline of faithful obedience to the Word? How do new, or young believers begin the process of encouraging their children to follow their example when they're still learning themselves? Don't panic! God doesn't require us to know it all and be perfectly practicing all truth before we begin to disciple our own children. He just asks us to be faithfully obedient to the truths He is revealing to us through His Word and through our interactions with older, more mature believers. I can't emphasize enough the importance of spending adequate time in the Word of God. As you interact with the scriptures and put into practice the truths you learn, you will be equipping yourself to lead your children and others. In addition, may I encourage you to seek out an older believer and ask them to spend time studying the Word and praying together? Don't wait for someone to ask, take the onus on yourself and begin the process of building a relationship with an older, wiser, faithfully walking follower of the Lord Jesus Christ.

In this book we will explore five ways we can pro-actively disciple our children: discipleship through the Word, prayer, fellowship, scripture memorization, and finally, service. Our children won't learn effectively that which we aren't practicing. My encouragement to you is to work as diligently at your own obedience to God as you would like your children to work at diligently following your example. One of the wonderful things about children is their innate ability to spot hypocrisy. If we are "talking the talk, without walking the walk," they will know it and they will despise us for our hypocrisy. Our commitment to daily growth, faithful obedience, confession of sin, and quick repentance and restoration, will demonstrate what walking with Christ "looks like" for the believer. We aren't called to be perfect, (good thing too, because that just isn't happening around here!) however, we are called to be faithful imitators of Christ. Not perfect, but forgiven!

Although all of our children need to learn and grow in all five of these areas, you will quickly begin to see that while some children show strength in studying and applying God's Word, other children in your family may show their greatest strengths in prayer or scripture memorization. Take advantage of these strengths and encourage each of your children to develop their own areas of leadership, within your home first, and then later in the church and your community. We'll discuss practical ways in each section to incorporate your children as co-teachers in those areas where they show particular gifts or diligence.

Sometimes it is easy as a mom and disciple-maker to work the hardest and do the most teaching in the areas that are the easiest for us, those areas of our own strength. I would encourage you to force yourself out of your own comfort zone and to give equal training and practice to each of these five key areas. One of the greatest benefits that I personally have received from discipling my children is the spiritual growth and conviction that the systematic teaching and habit building have brought into my own life.

For some of you, disciple making isn't the issue, preparing dinner is your weakest area! Again, we aren't called to be Pinterest -perfect chefs! Providing a warm atmosphere, delicious (but not fancy) food, and unity within family relationships isn't an impossible goal. It just takes practice and a commitment to the process. Trust me, I didn't enter marriage or parenthood with any particular skill set when it came to homemaking! What I learned came from books and older women... And boy oh boy, am I thankful for those exceedingly patient older women. Now, after 30 years of meal preparation, I've developed some easy recipes and comfy meals that will take the guesswork out of the dinner part of the dinner and discipleship equation.

Along the way, I will share with you many of our favorite family friendly recipes. Our dinner hours have different needs at different times, so I will include: meals to freeze ahead, slow-cooker meals, casserole and one-dish meals, and super simple family favorites. All of the recipes have been husband and kid tested and approved, I hope you'll enjoy them! The last section of recipes will be some fun recipes you can use to teach spiritual lessons. Hopefully, as you incorporate these recipes into your family times, they will become much-loved traditions for your children to anticipate each year.

Now, the foundation is laid, let's get started on the adventure of discipling our children with excellence and excitement!

LEADING YOUR CHILD TO CHRIST

Although we cannot start a relationship with Christ *for* our children, we can certainly plant the seeds and water the soil that will make that decision an easy one. Do your children see you exhibit joy in your own relationship with Christ? Do they see you excited about what the Lord is doing in your life and eager to follow His leading? Parents who love and submit to the Lord in their home will produce fertile ground for children who desire to love and serve the same Savior.

Honestly, if we don't exhibit joy and excitement about our own relationship with the Lord, why in the world would we expect our children to want that same type of relationship? I can say with all honesty, coming to a saving knowledge of Jesus

Christ is the best thing that ever happened in my life. I cannot even imagine where I would be and what my life would be like without Jesus! I know you feel the same. The challenge is letting those around us in on that little secret! Don't hide the joy of your salvation. The more we allow Jesus to occupy our thoughts and inhabit our conversations, the more our children will see just how essential He is to our lives... That's when they'll want to know more and we'll have the joy of sharing our Jesus with them!

Some people believe that young children cannot make an informed decision to accept Jesus Christ as their Savior. I would strongly disagree. Of my eight children, several of them trusted Christ for salvation at the age of four and have gone on into their teen years and early adulthood with no doubts regarding their salvation. Other children in our family were older when they committed themselves to the Lord, but they too have gone on in confidence, seeking to follow the Lord wholeheartedly. A few of my teens have had times of recommitment when they solidified their initial relationship with Christ. They felt the need to publicly and privately establish that their commitment to Christ was truly their own, not just a by-product of growing up in a Christian home. Both my husband and I encouraged them in those decisions. There is nothing more important to me than having my children recognize that their walk with the Lord is theirs and theirs alone. I want them to take ownership of their relationship with Christ in the same way I take ownership of my own relationship with Christ. Remember, it doesn't matter how much YOU love the Lord, unless your children experience their own salvation relationship with Jesus, they cannot be saved!

There is one common denominator in the salvation testimonies of all of my children. At the point that they were ready to be saved, they had no doubt about their own sinful condition. I have heard mothers tell their children, "Jesus loves you and wants you to be saved. Don't you want to get saved?" Although it is absolutely true that Jesus loves our children, this is an incomplete picture of what is necessary in salvation. Jesus does love our children, but He also hates their sin and cannot simply ignore it because of His great love for them.

Until a child is ready to acknowledge their own personal sin, they are not ready to receive Christ as their Savior. Acknowledgement of sin is not simply an admission that yes; everyone has sinned. Instead, acknowledgement of sin is a willingness to name their sin specifically and claim it as their own. For example: I lied, or I was unkind, or I stole that candy. Before they were ready to be saved, all of my children were more than eager to tell me that their brothers and sisters were sinners, but when it came to admitting their own sin, suddenly they went mute. At the point when they were truly ready to submit to Christ as their Lord and Savior, they were almost desperate to admit their sin to Him and be forgiven. Sometimes, when the floodgates of admission of sin burst open, I was surprised to realize just how much of what I considered "accidentally" naughty behavior was actually premeditated acts of defiance. As my children confessed those actions to the Lord, it was a good reminder to me that I needed to be more alert and aware of hidden attitudes in our home!

When a child understands their own personal sinfulness, they can then clearly understand their need for a Savior and in childlike faith receive Christ as their Lord and Savior. No, they won't necessarily understand all of the scriptural principles and implications inherent in salvation, but they can, in childlike faith, ask Jesus to forgive them for their sin and then, ask Him to come live in their heart as their Lord and Savior.

There is no magic prayer that will save your child. It can be as simple as them praying after you, or perhaps they will want to come up with their own prayer. Teach into the moment and show them how to seek forgiveness, repent, and receive Christ's forgiveness. For example, *"Dear God, please forgive me for lying, I know now that I am a sinner. Please come live in my heart and show me how to love and obey You. Thank you for dying on the cross for me. In Jesus name, Amen."*

After your child has prayed to become a Christian, I would strongly suggest making them a "birth certificate." On the certificate, include the date that they were saved, details about their salvation testimony, and then have anyone that was present sign the certificate as a witness. Should they have doubts when they are older because they cannot remember specifics of their salvation experience, the birth certificate will always be available as a reminder to jog their memory. Make sure they have their own bible and tape the birth certificate into the front cover. The certificate doesn't need to be elaborate or time consuming to produce. A simple hand written "birth certificate" will be just as precious to your child as an ornately produced certificate.

Remind your child that now that they belong to Jesus, He will never ever leave them. Use scriptures such as Hebrews 13:5, "for He Himself has said, I will never leave you nor forsake you," and I John 5:13, "These things I have written to you who believe in the name of the Son of God, in order that you may know that you have eternal life," to remind your child that his/her salvation is permanent. In the same way that they didn't earn salvation by their good behavior, they won't lose their salvation when they once again choose bad behavior.

Be the historian for your child. As they mature, remind them of the fruit that is evident in their life since their salvation. Keep a written reminder of how and when they became a Christian for yourself, so that you don't forget the details. Perhaps you will want to celebrate their spiritual birthday in a special way. Take the time to help your children remember all that led up to their salvation.

Prior to our children's salvation, any work of discipleship that we do will be an investment in preparing them for their own future relationship with Christ. We fill the position of a faithful seed-planter. After salvation, that discipleship takes on a whole new dimension and excitement. Now you can teach and relate to your child not only as a parent, but also as a sister or brother in Christ. To echo the Apostle John, " I have no greater joy than this, to hear of my children walking in truth." (3 John 1:4)

DISCIPLING OUR CHILDREN WITH THE WORD

D o you love the Word of God? Do you obey the Word of God? Do your children know that you love and obey the Word of God? Our attitude toward the authority and importance of the Scriptures will be the greatest influence on how our children view God's Word. Your example in reading the Word, sharing what you have learned from the Word, and consistently obeying the Word, will do more to influence your children than anything you simply tell them about their own need for scripture reading.

Before my children were born, I delighted in spending extensive amounts of time reading the Word of God. I was a fairly new believer and I just couldn't seem to get my fill of the scriptures.

I rose early and often stayed up late just to read and make more notes about what I was reading. Then... I had children. Oh sure, I was still getting up early, but it wasn't to spend time in the Word, it was to placate a squalling baby. I was staying up late, but it wasn't to meditate and memorize, it was to again placate that squalling baby. I longed for my relaxed and easily planned time in the Word and honestly, sometimes I sulked because I wasn't getting what I wanted. Something needed to change. Actually, *someone* needed to change and that someone was me! I began to find ways to slip more time in the Word into my day. Instead of sitting for hours with my bible, prayer list, and notebook, I kept a bible open on the kitchen counter so that when I passed by my eyes could stop and take in a tidbit of scripture. I began to post little "scripture notes" on mirrors and windowsills so that my eyes would notice and my heart would be filled. Instead of bemoaning the time I didn't have, I tried to make the most of the time I could manufacture. Although this wasn't my goal, as my children began to grow older, they grew up seeing mom always looking at her scripture. They saw that the Word of God was so important to me that I was always finding a way to absorb it. Obviously, as my children grew older I also found more time to immerse myself in scripture, but I still maintained the habit of keeping what I was reading out for them to see. When all of our devotional time with the Lord is behind closed doors, we rob our children of the valuable opportunity to see us interacting with the Word of God. It is important for them to observe that we don't just say that our family needs to be in the Word, we actually make that time a priority in our own lives. Another bonus of having my bible out and available came in its daily use as a counselor and tool of correction and encouragement. Because my bible was, and still is, out all day, when issues arose in our home, I had the Word of God to turn to as my authority.

I always tried to give my children biblical counsel and encouragement, but my best efforts pale in comparison to allowing the Word of God to speak counsel and encouragement into their lives and the situations they encounter.

From the time that our children were little, we told them that someday they would learn to read. We didn't encourage them that they would learn to read to catch up with the latest popular book or to read magazines or newspapers. Instead, we encouraged them that they would learn to read so that they could read God's Word for themselves. Because we were excited about that future goal, all of our children became excited as well. True to our word, as soon as they were reading at a second grade level, we purchased them their own leather bound bible with their name imprinted on the front. What a treasure! They couldn't wait to be like us and carry their own bible to church in order to follow along with the scripture reading. Are you building that kind of excitement in your children's lives? You are the cheerleader for spiritual things and they will take their cues from you.

This is definitely a personal family decision, but I always encouraged my children to underline and write notes in their new leather bibles. My own bible is well worn and full of dates, underlined scriptures, and helpful personal notes. When I open my bible, I have a written record of how the Word of God, through the influence of the Holy Spirit, has shaped and changed me. I can look at certain dates linked with certain scriptures and see areas of growth and conviction. Often, the notes I jotted down 10 years ago still bring the same comfort or encouragement I needed when I wrote them down so many years before. I want my children to experience that same blessing and to have the same attachment to their bibles. In fact, my kids joke that I love my bible so much that should our home catch on fire I'd be torn over whom to rescue first... them or my precious bible. (It would be them, of course, but I like to keep them guessing!)

Disclaimer: Don't expect that the leather bible you purchase for your new readers will be the leather bible they use for the rest of their lives! If you can discard that expectation, you can free them up to mark their bibles with joy and abandon. My oldest two children took bible highlighting to a new level. I gave each of them a colored highlighter and instructed them to underline everything they read in their bibles that was important to them. This instruction came after years of teaching them that every word in the bible was specifically chosen by God and was there for our good and our growth. Guess what they did? They underlined every word in their bibles because obviously, every word was important! How could I argue with that logic?

Before they ever knew Jesus as their personal Savior, however, we spent time immersing our children in the scriptures. Many times, actions precede belief. In the area of bible reading and daily time in the Word, I didn't want to wait until my children professed faith in Christ to begin the habit of daily devotions. In fact, scripture makes it clear that God's Word is much better at bringing conviction for sin than I am. Allowing the scripture to talk to my children's hearts took me out of the picture and reminded them that their sin struggle was with the God of the universe... Not the mom they faced across the kitchen table. At different times we used different types of bibles and bible storybooks, but the children always knew that the Word of God was central to our lives and actions. They knew that as much as possible, I tried to base my decisions concerning them on the Word of God and they also knew that when I was unsure of what to do, I stopped and took the time to pray and search the scriptures for my answers.

When all of the children were young, we read each day from the Egermeier's Bible Story book. I would highly recommend this book for all families. The bible stories were not dumbed down in any way and my husband and I often found ourselves reaching for our own bibles to see where the explicit details were found. Because of the amazing detail found in the Egermeier's, my older children still to this day, have very specific and detailed bible knowledge that is remarkable. I especially appreciated that the Egermeier Bible storybook didn't commentate on the scripture. It just told the stories as recorded in the Bible and allowed the Holy Spirit to do the work of commentating.

Along with the scriptures, we also used a simple catechism book while the children were young. As they learned and memorized doctrinal truths, we would look up the scriptures that verified those truths. Those memorized catechisms proved helpful to my college aged children when they were defending their faith and needed to remember where certain truths were found in the bible. However, simply reading the bible is not enough for our children. We need to take the truths that we are reading and find ways to make them real in our children's lives.

For example, when we learned that God is the Creator, it was important to make opportunities to show our children the creative power of God. This was done so simply as we walked through the woods or in the backyard. Turning over rocks to see the bugs underneath, collecting leaves of myriad types, watching the seasons change, catching fireflies, studying the stars, all of these activities gave our children the opportunity to see the Creator God in action.

As often as possible, we need to make scripture real and relevant for our children. As we point out answers to prayer, our children see the faithfulness of God. As we thank God for protection after a trip, they begin to realize that God watches over them, even when they are not aware of His presence. Use every opportunity you can find to bring God's Word to life. At first, this continual conversing about God may seem unnatural or stilted. However, the more we talk about God, the more we will see Him in our everyday activities, and the more He will become a normal and natural part of our conversations. It's beautiful to talk to children who have grown up in a home where God is always part of the conversation. They speak of the Lord as easily and affectionately as they would speak of their mother, father, or siblings.

As soon as our children were beginner readers, but not yet ready for their own leather bible, I would buy them a Beginners Bible and make them a daily devotional notebook. The Beginner's Bible is so simply written that early readers can read a story a day with little or no trouble. I would buy the children a special notebook and write one question per day in the notebook, which corresponded with their reading for the day. Spelling didn't matter and some of the children's answers to the questions were just priceless. After reading about Jesus choosing His 12 disciples, one of my children wrote in her notebook about Jesus and the 12 *recycles*! Of course we laughed at the time, but isn't that quite a true picture of what happened to the disciple's hearts...they were recycled into something new and wonderful!

As more of our children grew older and we had fewer tiny babies, we switched to daily reading from our own bibles. The readers would each take a turn reading aloud and then we would discuss what we had read. Although it is tempting to use bible reading time to address pressing discipline issues, resist the urge! Our goal is to teach our children to love the Word, not to use it as a club over their heads. Use another time to take them to the Word for correction and instruction! For struggling readers, choose short verses or passages that they can competently handle without embarrassment. Spend time encouraging their efforts and you will observe them growing in confidence with each daily time of reading.

To help our children cement the habit of daily bible reading, we had each of the children read the Proverb of the day, (there are 31 Proverbs, one for each day) and then they wrote their favorite verse from that Proverb on a color-coded 3x5 card, which was placed in a basket in the kitchen. At the end of the month, we separated the cards by color and discussed why some of the verses were chosen. This is something in which the whole family could participate. The children know that I am spending time in the Word, but seeing me deposit my card in the basket was a secure reminder that we were all in this growth process together.

Always take the time to discuss what you read together in scripture. Many times I have assumed that the children understood what we were reading, but our discussions showed me otherwise. The goal is not simply that our children know bible stories and facts, but that they can take the Word of God, apply it to their lives, and live a life characterized by obedience to the Lord Jesus Christ. Be careful not to allow your children to coast by with "religious" answers to your questions. Dig deeper and help them recognize when they are simply accomplishing head learning without incorporating and seeking for heart change!

To help my children remember what we had read in our bible times, I often used the drive to church as a review of the week's reading. I would begin a narration like this..."Saul was the

King of the Israelites, he wasn't God's choice, but the people chose him because he was"... then a child would continue with the narration for a few sentences until I passed it on to the next child, then the next, and so on. Often I was surprised by the details my children remembered and sometimes, as they added personal commentary to the story, (i.e. David was brave just like Daddy!) I would springboard off what they said to expand our teaching.

Many times, as we were sitting around the dinner table, we would review an entire month of bible reading from memory. I would narrate what we had read and the children would add the details they saw that I was missing. It was fun to see which children found certain things too important to be left out. Everyone was able to participate and this was such a normal routine for our family that we never really had a problem with anyone not cooperating. However, if someone did seem uninvolved, it was a red flag for me to check up on what was going on with that child personally. It is important for our children to see the bible as one cohesive whole, instead of many stand alone stories. This practice of review and narration helped to build the important habit of always examining the scripture in context. As the children grew older and began to work on their own bible studies, the habit of looking to see the context of what they were studying was a huge help to them.

Another simple tool to help your children learn to recognize contextual tools as they begin to study their own bibles, is teaching them to recognize just WHOM the scripture is referring to in each passage. In a notebook, simply have your children write the words God, Jesus, and Holy Spirit down the left hand side of a page. Then, as they read, have them make a tally mark for each time there is a reference to one of the members of the Godhead. After they have completed their daily reading, have them add up the totals for each. This simple visual will help them to recognize whether the passage is talking about God the Father, Jesus the Savior and Son, or the Holy Spirit who intercedes for us. This contextual understanding will open up the scriptures to their young minds and help them as they grow in their relationships with Christ.

A great way to help incorporate biblical truths into your children's lives is through the use of hymns. The old hymns are jam-packed full of doctrinal truths and scriptural references. As our children sing, "Great is Thy faithfulness, Oh God my Father..." they are reminded of their relationship with their heavenly Father. In the same way, as they sing "How Great Thou Art," they can understand more clearly the awesome nature of our God. A family hymnal is a worthwhile investment that will be used over and over again for years. Although we love and sing scripture songs and praise choruses, there is something special about the depth and character of the old hymns of the faith. Trust me, I'm not a great singer, but singing the hymns with my children is one of my favorite things to do! For my youngest children, I often called the church secretary to find out what hymns would be sung on the next Sunday. I then picked one of the hymns to practice each day during the week. By Sunday, even my smallest children could participate in the worship as they sang along with an already well-known, (to them,) hymn. As the weeks passed, their arsenal of memorized hymns grew and they felt intimately connected with the adults as we all worshipped together.

Along with their personal daily bible reading, we also sometimes provided devotional materials to complement the children's reading. Many such devotional materials are available today. I would caution you to always pre-read the devotional books that you give to your children. Although they may be "popular" with all of your children's friends, or the newest book on the market, they may not enforce the standard of belief and conduct that you are trying to teach your children. Keep looking, there are many great devotional books available, we just need to be wise in choosing the right devotional for the right child.

Here is an important reminder: just because a book was helpful for one of your children, doesn't necessarily mean that it is a good choice for another child in your family! Different personalities, different sin appetites, and different levels of maturity must all be considered as we make these books available to our children. Remember, once **you** have placed a devotional book into your child's hand the assumption of that child is that you are endorsing what is written inside. It is much harder to un-teach bad doctrine or loose spiritual standards than it is to make wise choices in the beginning.

Don't limit yourself by only incorporating "age appropriate" devotional materials. Although my children have enjoyed some of the simpler devotional books, they have also loved and used and re-used books such as *My Utmost For His Highest*, by Oswald Chambers and *Streams in the Desert* by L. Cowan.

Although complementary devotional materials are a helpful addition to our children's daily devotional times, they should never replace daily bible reading. Be observant. If your child is faithfully reading the supplemental materials, but skipping their actual bible reading, it is time to give the devotional materials a break.

One easy way to establish a faithful habit of morning devotions is through instituting a "No Bible-No

Breakfast" policy. Although we don't always have this policy in effect, when we do it is a powerful impetus to remind every family member of the importance of starting his or her day in the scriptures. Perhaps, I'm the one who needs the "No Bible-No Breakfast" rule the most! Without it, it's easy for the needs of the moment to take precedent over the spiritual needs of growth and maturity.

One of the special things I did for our older children was to create their own daily flip calendar with devotional bible reading and commentary by Mom. I took 3x5 cards and attached them at the top with locking rings. On the cards I wrote a daily bible verse with a short encouragement about the verse. I didn't choose verses because I was trying to get a point across to that particular child, but instead I tried to fill the calendar with important doctrinal verses and encouraging verses about God's strength, holiness, mercy, and great love toward them. About every 15 days, they would find a card instructing them to come share a memory verse with me and receive a treat from me. This is an ongoing project since I still have younger children at home. My prayer has always been that this keepsake would be an encouragement that my children could keep and return to during times of discouragement or loneliness.

At times, I used a simple sticker chart to encourage faithfulness in daily Bible reading. Each day that a child completed their personal devotions, they could stick a sticker on the chart. When all of the children had together filled the chart, we then had a special family treat. Making the reward contingent on completion by all of the children created an atmosphere of positive peer pressure that encouraged the less eager devotional readers.

Since I wrote the first edition of this book, times have changed. I have entered, albeit reluctantly, this new age of technology. With new technology has come new ways of interacting with both the Word of God and my children. Now, I can use my smart phone to encourage them with the Word. Often, after I have my morning time in the Word, I will send all of my children a verse or two to start their day off with scripture. Again, I don't try to find verses that will scold or convict them into living the way I think they should live! Instead, I try to share verses that will give them hope, peace, and joy throughout their day. I don't just include my own children in this practice. I also send texts to the new children I have gained through my son and daughter's marriages, as well as some young adults who consider me as "mom." I know that I could send the scripture out as a group text, (if I could ever figure out group texting,) but sending each text individually allows me to personalize the scripture when I sense a certain young adult needs a specific word of encouragement. As well, it makes it possible for them to send back any prayer need they are facing without the entire group being privy to their message.

Use your imagination and ask God to show you ways that you can make His Word and daily time in the Word not only a habit, but also a delight for both you and your children. II Timothy 3:16-17 tells us, "All scripture is inspired by God and profitable for teaching, for reproof, for correction, for training in righteousness; that the man of God may be adequate, equipped for every good work." In other words, for everything you need in life, God has graciously given us His Word. How amazing that He has entrusted to us the task of passing on a love for that Word to our children.

> *"Everything you need in life, God has graciously given us His Word."*

TEACHING CHILDREN TO PRAY

*"Prayer does not change God, but
it changes him who prays."*
–Soren Kierkegaard

The second area of discipleship in which we must train our children is the discipline of prayer. Our goal should be children who have a consistent and persistent relationship of prayer with their God.

We want to see our children changed to be more like Christ as they turn their hearts toward Him in prayer. We must teach our children that prayer isn't simply approaching God with our list of wants and desires; rather, prayer is a continual conversation of talking and listening to our God. As with all other areas of discipleship, this doesn't just happen. It takes continual patient modeling and teaching from us, and purposeful times of practice throughout our children's days.

In the beginning, before they have their own personal relationship with Christ, the purpose of teaching your children to pray is to build the foundational practice of prayer into their lives. From their earliest days, we want our children to know that they have a heavenly Father who desires to hear and respond to their prayers. Actually, He isn't just willing to hear our prayers; we serve a God who is *eagerly* waiting for us to come to Him in humble reliance. Obviously, this truth will take on a whole new dimension when your child has accepted Jesus Christ as their personal Savior, but don't wait until that day to begin training them to pray! Long before your infant realizes that you are praying with him, you can fold his tiny hands and pray as you lay him down for bedtime and naps. When your toddler is eating meals in the highchair take a few moments to help them fold their hands and bow their heads as you thank the Lord for their food.

Our children's days offer us many opportunities to pray with, for, and about them. Do your children know that you pray for them? Often, our own personal prayer times are private, and although we tell our children that we pray for them, they never actually witness us praying. I would encourage you to occasionally pray for them in an open area. Perhaps you could ask them for any pressing prayer needs and then stop and pray for them right then and there. It builds security in our children's lives when they see us praying for them and taking their needs before the throne of God. As they see us modeling the practice of prayer, they will begin to incorporate that same practice into their own lives. I want my children to know that for me, prayer isn't a last resort, but it's the first place I run with my fears, needs, and joys.

Many of the times of prayer that I will be sharing will be most effectively learned through observation, not simply through verbal teaching. As your children see you praying in these different times and situations, they will naturally begin to turn to prayer at those times as well. It's one thing to tell our children how important prayer is and how they should consistently pray; it's another thing altogether to model the practice of prayer and to eagerly share our delight in the answers to prayer that we receive from God. Quite honestly, when I realized how important my own model of prayer was to my children's spiritual growth, I experienced a revitalization of my own prayer life. The need to model consistency in prayer caused me to be consciously aware of how persistent I was in running to the Lord with my prayer concerns. Sometimes, my children have become my greatest teachers! Becoming persistent and consistent in my prayers has been a continual learning process for me. For years, I beat myself up because I didn't feel as though I ever spent as much concentrated time in prayer, as I should. I burdened myself with expectations of a neatly organized prayer journal and hours spent alone in my prayer closet. Prayer became a guilty thought that I avoided because I was convinced that I was a praying failure. *I was wrong!* As I've grown and matured in my own personal walk with the Lord, I've realized more clearly what it means to be in constant communication with my Lord through prayer. I slip into prayer so quickly now that sometimes, I don't even realize that I'm praying for the first few moments. Prayer isn't something I have to do; rather it's a continual conversation with the Lover of my soul and Protector of my heart. Yes, I do have a prayer journal and yes, I do try to have a somewhat systematic plan in my prayer life, but it is my spontaneous and intimate conversations with Jesus that bring me the most peace, comfort, security, direction, and conviction. Realizing that the Lord wasn't watching me to see how often I failed, but patiently waiting for me to run to Him so that He could share His heart and love with me was a real turning point in both my prayer life and my walk with the Lord. Are you burdened by feelings of failure concerning your lack of prayer? Please, don't be! God doesn't despise your small efforts of coming to Him in prayer. Instead, He delights in communicating with you and He's aching to bless your smallest acts of obedience!

For one entire year, I designated one day of the week as a special day of prayer for our family. I bought a notebook with dividers and the night before my prayer day each week, I would place the notebook on the kitchen counter. My children and husband knew that I would be praying diligently for their needs the next day and the notebook provided a handy place for them to record their prayer requests and for me to note the answers that the Lord provided. This discipline of concentrated prayer each week brought such sweet results, not only in answered prayers, but also in my relationships with each of the children and my husband. Although I haven't continued this practice on a weekly basis, I still set aside special days that I devote to praying for my family. I try to seek out each family member before that day to understand their prayer needs in order to pray effectively for them. Obviously, I also have some regular prayer subjects that always get covered such as my children's spiritual growth, safety, discernment, future (and now actual) spouses, friendships, and more.

When your children first awaken in the morning is a great time to start their day with prayer. Teach your children to thank God for a good night's sleep, (they'll understand when they are grown just what a blessing that is!), for the start of a new day, and for all of the activities that the day will hold for them. Often, when one of my children was struggling in a certain area, we would start the day praying for a willing heart to obey God and mommy in that area all day. I believe that as we pray for our children to stand strong in obedience, we help them build the confidence and strength they must have in order to obey in their hearts and actions.

Meals are another natural time to teach prayer. Be careful, our mealtime prayers can become so rote and routine that they are just filler and a daily repetition of the same words. My children had begun to joke that they could tell how hungry I was by how quickly I ended our breakfast prayer. Not so funny! I had to examine my own heart and consider the lesson I was passing on to my children. I want them to learn thankfulness and gratitude to God for the bountiful food He has blessed our family with, not that prayer is just something to get through quickly to get to the meal.

When my husband was not home, I often had my oldest son take his place in leading the rest of our family in mealtime prayers. This bestowed responsibility helped him to embrace his role as the oldest brother, and then extended beyond mealtime into his relationships with his younger siblings. When dad was home, many times it was the youngest child who was clamoring for the privilege to lead in prayer. By the time my sons were young men they were confident in leading prayer. May I share a secret? When a young man who is interested in our daughter first comes to our home to share a meal, my husband always asks him to lead the family in the mealtime prayer. For some young men this request is no problem. For some others, however, being asked to lead in prayer has caused consternation and embarrassment. Now, being able to lead in prayer obviously isn't the only requirement to pursue our daughters, but it does give us a starting point in evaluating a potential suitor's familiarity with

God. I've always tried to teach all my children, but especially my boys, that prayer is about talking to God, not about worrying if those listening are impressed by what they're hearing. In other words, it's not about what you say; it's about the connection of relationship with the Lord.

Another time to take advantage of the opportunity to teach prayer is during the family devotional time. We have approached prayer many different ways throughout the years. Sometimes when we are praying, we just pray around the circle, praying for the person sitting to our left. We always encourage our children to share their prayer needs and then we can help the youngest children remember what to pray for their person. At other times, we would start with the youngest and have him pray for the next oldest sibling, and up, and up the list until Dad, who would then close the loop by praying for the youngest child.

The Word of God gives us very clear direction
concerning qualities that we, as families, can
always pray for one another with confidence.
Consider Ephesians 1:16-19:

> *(Paul) Do not cease giving thanks for you, while*
> *making mention of you in my prayers: that*
> *the God of our Lord Jesus Christ, the Father of*
> *glory, may give to you a spirit of wisdom and of*
> *revelation in the knowledge of Him. I pray that*
> *they eyes of your heart may be enlightened,*
> *so that you may know what is the hope of*
> *His calling, what are the riches of the glory of*
> *His inheritance in the saints, and what is the*
> *surpassing greatness of His power toward us who*
> *believe. These are in accordance with the working*
> *of the strength of His might.*

As we observe this scripture, we can learn what
Paul considered important in his prayers for the
church at Ephesus. He prayed that they would

have a spirit of wisdom. Isn't that what we want for our children, wisdom to navigate the many decisions they will encounter in their lives? He prayed that they would have knowledge of God, that is my deepest prayer for my children, that they would know God fully and intimately. He prayed that they might know the hope of their calling, so too, our children need to know that hope when times are difficult or God seems distant. Finally, Paul prayed that the church would know the riches of the glory of His inheritance and the greatness of His power toward believers. I want my children to know the deep, deep love that God shows to those who are His! All of these truths are wonderful things to pray for one another in our families.

Let's look a bit further in scripture and consider Colossians 1:9-12:

> *For this reason also, since the day we heard of it, we have not ceased to pray for you and to ask*

*that you may be filled with the knowledge of His
will in all spiritual wisdom and understanding,
so that you may walk in a manner worthy of
the Lord, to please Him in all respects, bearing
fruit in every good work and increasing in the
knowledge of God; strengthened with all power,
according to His glorious might, for the attaining
of all steadfastness and patience; joyously giving
thanks to the Father, who has qualified us to
share in the inheritance of the saints in light.*

Although there is some repetition from
Ephesians 1, we also see an expansion of the
qualities that we can pray for our children and
that they, in turn, can pray for us. We can pray
for one another that we would walk in a manner
that pleases the Lord; this one simple concept
encompasses all areas of our lives. We can pray
for one another that we would bear good fruit.
We can pray for our children and they can pray
for us and for one another that we would gain

steadfastness, patience, and joyful hearts, full of thanksgiving.

Allow me to share one more scripture with you. There are times that we must be away from our children. In fact, I would urge you to occasionally plan times away that are just for mom and dad; times that you can shed your parental roles and remember how to be best friends and lovers once more! During those times, my greatest distraction was concern about how the children were treating one another. Without me there, were they still being kind, tenderhearted, and merciful to one another? As I prayed about my concerns and prayed for my children, the Lord gave me these verses. I printed them out and taped them to the refrigerator. Before traveling, I would remind my children that this was my prayer for them. I encouraged them to refer to the verse when they were tempted to speak sharply or to become frustrated with a younger sibling. As always,

God's Word was able to provide a safeguard and accountability in ways that I couldn't self-produce. Here is the passage:

Ephesians 4:2-3
Be completely humble and gentle; be patient, bearing with one another in love. Make every effort to keep the unity of the Spirit through the bond of peace.

There you have it. Everything I wanted my children to embody to one another all wrapped up in one verse! I knew that if my children could be humble, patient, gentle, and unified, they would be able to bear with one another's shortcomings; even when the toddler was annoying, the older brother was bossy, the sister's were emotional, and everyone missed mom! God's Word became our family prayer and it beautifully accomplished God's purposes. Take some time to teach these concepts to your children. Too often, our times of prayer become nothing more than lists of "wants" that we are presenting to God. Instead, as we pray for these godly character qualities to be evident in our lives more and more each day, we begin to see God molding us to be more like Christ. This isn't just about our children. Praying with our children about Godly character will change us, as well. And, when our children see us begin to change, they will be encouraged that they can change, too. Remember, prayer doesn't change God; it changes us!

Teaching our children to pray gives us wonderful opportunities to enlarge their world. As we pray for friends and relatives who are living far away, and missionaries both here and abroad, we give our children the ability to see how God works far away, while we pray here. Teach your children to pray for needs at home, in their community, in their country, and in their world. That type of prayer is Great Commission oriented and will keep our hearts focused outwardly. Don't worry, God knows our personal needs and he won't forget to care for us, as we are busy praying for Him to meet the needs of others!

There are so many ways to teach this heart of prayer to your children. At different times we have used some or all of the following ideas. Missionary prayer cards provide a great visual reminder to your children of who exactly it is that they are praying for. Look for prayer requests and prayer updates at your church to keep your prayers for the missionaries fresh and up to date. More and more missionaries and ministries can be found online. As you follow Facebook statuses, tweets, Instagram photos, and blog posts, you will find "at the moment" needs to pray for and blessings in which you can rejoice. You may want to get a good world map or globe in order to be able to show your children where exactly the missionaries are in reference to your own home. Use your map to help your children see the regions of the world that are undergoing hardships such as wars, famine, diseases, and poverty. Understanding the needs of others will help our children develop gratitude for all they have so bountifully received.

When we received Christmas cards each year, we kept the pictures that came with many of those cards and placed them in a basket on our dining room table. For those cards that did not have a picture, we cut off the back of the card with the sender's name on it, and placed those in the basket as well. For the weeks leading up to Christmas and until New Years, we would each pull a card or picture from the basket at dinnertime and pray for the family or person represented. I pointed out to the children that if those people cared enough about us to remember us with a card, the least we could do to show our appreciation was to remember them to God in prayer. One year, just to mix things up a bit, I took giant pieces of poster board and cut out large wreath shapes. We then stapled the Christmas card pictures to the wreath shapes and hung them in the dining room. Each night we prayed for the families smiling down at us from the wall. Either way, my children were able to put faces with prayer requests and it made prayer just that much more real to them.

Another tool we used to stimulate prayer was a simple filing tab. These are available at office stores or department stores. What I'm describing are the round white tags with metal around the edge. We wrote the name of a different person or organization on each tag and stored them in a glass jar. Every day, we would each pull a tag from the jar and during our bible time we would pray for whoever or whatever was written on the tag. The tag was then deposited in another glass jar. When all of the tags moved from one jar to the other, we celebrated with ice cream sundaes. Then, we began all over again. I kept a supply of blank tags, so that when we made new friends or heard of new prayer needs, I could quickly add another tag to the jar. Once a week, I would have the children write a letter to one of the people they had prayed for that week. Often, they would share with people at church the fact that they had been prayed for during the week. For my youngest children, they only knew some of the people they prayed for through the tags, but they still felt a relationship with them through praying for them.

For our older children's personal times of prayers, I bought them each a spiral bound set of 3x5 cards. On each of these cards they wrote a different prayer concern. For example, some cards contained family member names or friend's names, while other cards contained the names of ministries or groups for whom they had committed to pray. As they prayed, they could flip through the cards therefore making sure no one was forgotten. One child carried these cards in her backpack and pulled them out when she was riding in the car or just had a time of waiting before an activity. The cards kept prayer requests organized and easily accessible. Having the cards in her backpack also provided a constant reminder to pray. It's no surprise to me that she is my child with the strongest prayer life.

These are some of the planned times of prayer that we incorporated as a family. However, often prayer is a spontaneous "need of the moment," activity. As we passed accidents on the road, I would ask for one or more of the children to volunteer to pray for the victims and emergency workers. As we heard on the news of a natural disaster or some other tragedy, I would gather the children and take time to pray. When the children were small and would hurt themselves, a band-aid took care of the physical need, but prayer was what took care of the heart hurt. It was always encouraging for me to see an older child stopping to pray with a younger child that had fallen and was crying. I knew the children were catching our model of prayer when I began to observe them stopping regularly to pray with their friends. Even as small children, they learned that bringing God into a situation was always the right choice.

As my children became teenagers, prayer became an even more important tool in my parenting toolbox. Regardless of their maturity, regardless of their spiritual life, regardless of their even-keeled temperament, for teenagers, too much of their life is just filled to overflowing with DRAMA. Often, praying with the kids was the only thing that could help them to put everything into perspective. When they felt that I just couldn't understand what they were going through, bringing God into the conversation through prayer, reminded them that they had a Father who always understood.

As important as it is for us to be praying *for* our children's future spouses, when they become teens I think it's just as important for us to be praying *with* them about that all-important topic. Praying together about the young people they met and began to consider as future mates kept the lines of communication open and discouraged secrecy. When they were able to pray *with* me about their friends and when they knew I upheld their friends *for* them, my teens were more open to hearing my legitimate concerns about their friends' actions or attitudes. Many times, my teens shared things with me during our prayer times that they were nervous about sharing in an eye-to-eye, face-to-face conversation. Prayer provided a way for them to open the window of their heart without fear of condemnation or an immediate scolding.

One simple way to begin to build these times of "open window" prayer sharing is by instituting prayer walks with your children. Although I haven't used this tool with all of my children, for some, a prayer walk is just the right choice when it comes to initiating times of prayer and sharing. What's a prayer walk? A prayer walk is simply a time that I ask one child to join me in praying and walking. As we walk, I will begin praying and pray for a few minutes about whatever the Lord lays on my heart. After a few minutes, I stop praying and the teen begins to pray. They pray for a time and then I begin to pray again. We continue this way until the walk is done.

A prayer walk produces such wonderful fruit in my relationships with my teens. The great teachers of the past, such as Socrates and Aristotle, used to teach their students by walking and talking with them. There is just something about side-by-side walking that opens doors of communication and breaks down walls of resistance. As we walked and prayed together, I didn't have to pry into what was happening in my children's lives. I didn't have to ask them what they were excited about, or fearful about, or what they were concerned about for their friends, those things just spilled out naturally in prayer. Sometimes, after the walk I would ask some clarifying questions, but generally speaking, I just took their concerns to heart and began to pray for their heart issues, now with a clearer understanding. For one daughter who particularly struggled with communicating with me during her teen years, those prayer walks kept our relationship intact in the midst of her somewhat tumultuous transition to adulthood.

I must add one word of caution here. If your child shares something about a friend, (or themselves) that is illegal, dangerous, or that will cause lifelong consequences, it is your responsibility to get involved! I didn't say it was your responsibility to flip out, freak out, or over-react... However, as a mature adult, assure your teen that you will help them walk through the situation, but let them know that the consequences are too big for them to carry alone. Do whatever it takes to minister in a calm, loving manner. (Did I mention calm? No freaking out!) If you overreact and cause more drama, your teen will withdraw and close and lock the window of their heart. Don't do it! When they see that we can be trusted to handle their prayers with a loving and Christ-like empathy, they will trust us with their hearts.

Our children have always observed me stopping to pray with people, whether it is in person or over the phone. Because that practice is so ingrained in their lives, I have been blessed as they often call home from college simply asking me to take a moment and pray with them. My now married children have become some of my dearest prayer partners as we continue to pray with and for one another. My children are all confident that we pray for them, but when they are far from home there is something very comforting and secure about having us pray with them. I have been very encouraged to see them do the same for one another and for their friends. Often, I will walk into a bedroom to find one of my children with their eyes closed, praying over the phone with a friend. One daughter, in particular, has become the "go to" person for prayer among her friends. What a great reputation to have and what a wonderful opportunity she has found to minister to her hurting friends.

When I was still a young believer, I was strongly convicted that if I told someone that I was praying for them, I had better be doing it! It became very clear to me that to say I was praying, and then not to pray, was nothing less than a lie. I hated the feeling of guilt I would experience when I would run into someone I had promised to pray for and then, I would suddenly remember that I had not fulfilled that promise. Because of this conviction in my heart, I have tried to make it a practice to pray immediately with people when they mention a prayer concern. I have also passed this teaching on to my children. We have talked often about the need to follow through on our promises to pray and how to do otherwise is deceitful and makes us hypocrites. Because of this teaching, all of my children are quick to pray with their siblings, their friends, and with us, their parents.

Praying alone will come easily for most of your children. Although they will need training and reminders to make prayer a habitual practice, praying alone isn't intimidating. However, praying out loud is a different story and for some children will only become easier as they are encouraged to practice group prayer. Do not allow your children to refuse to pray out loud. You will be doing them a great disservice as they build a deep-seated habit of refusal to obey God in prayer. Instead, help them choose one thing to pray about and then, calmly and consistently insist that they join the family in prayer. When I was a new believer in college, I read the Lord's Prayer out loud in prayer meeting after prayer meeting until I gained the confidence to pray about the requests that were being shared. Corporate prayer is a learned habit that is best taught in the security of your own home. Make the most of your opportunities to teach this important discipline. Again, remind your children that they are praying to an audience of One, and that audience is the Lord. It really, truly doesn't matter what anyone "thinks" of their prayer; instead, it's all about communication with the God Whom delights in His relationship with them!

To keep prayer fresh for your children, sometimes change the format. We have had times of prayer that we didn't pray for any specific requests, but simply went around the prayer circle thanking God for everything He brought to our minds. As you can imagine, some of these prayer times were quite long! We have had times of prayer that were simply spent repeating back to God the attributes that describe His character. We have had times that the entire family simply prayed for or gave thanks for one individual family member. There are so many different aspects of prayer; they are just as varied and unique as our unique God. Don't allow prayer to become boring, rote, or uninteresting. Ask God to show you how to make prayer one of the sweetest parts of your family heritage.

There have been times when my husband and I have had to make major decisions and we have entered a time of fasting and prayer. We taught into those times with our children and shared with them how God could use our sacrifice from meals to speak to our hearts more clearly. Often, the children would ask to join us in fasting. Children are not physically ready for extended fasts, but we would allow them to skip one meal and we would spend that mealtime praying as a family. They learned what it felt like to sacrifice something for

God, and even more importantly, they learned that they were an integral part of our family prayers for God's direction. Please be careful and evaluate **your** children's health needs before you let them skip a meal, all of my children are very healthy with no blood sugar issues, so I knew that one meal wouldn't harm them. More and more, recently, I find myself choosing to fast from technology, or more specifically, social media, when I need to focus on specific prayer needs. Taking the time away from the all-consuming Internet helps me to tune out the distractions of the everyday world and focus closely on what God is trying to impress on my heart. When I am captivated by the earthly, (as found in my newsfeed) I struggle to focus on the eternal...

Don't be taken by surprise as you see your children beginning to incorporate prayer into more and more parts of their daily life. When our daughter, Emma, was in the 2-3 year old Sunday school class, each week there was one little girl who entered the class sobbing uncontrollably for her mommy. No amount of teacher reassurance could calm this little girl. One Sunday, unprompted by us, Emma entered her classroom, walked over to the little girl, knelt beside her, and laid her hand on her shoulder and prayed for her to feel safe and be happy. She stayed beside her little friend until the sobs had subsided and then, she and the little girl walked hand in hand to the classroom table. The teacher was stunned and quite honestly so were we! Shame on us! Prayer was already such a natural part of Emma's life and she was so confident that God was eager to hear and answer her prayers that she immediately went to Him for help, fully trusting that He would hear and answer. Another time, when we had just come forward to be welcomed as new members of a church, the Pastor asked for a volunteer to close the service in prayer. Imagine our surprise when our four–year-old son Peter raised his hand.

I flinched, expecting a "thank you for this food" prayer, but Peter was already a confident prayer warrior and he closed the service with unexpected poise for a four-year-old.

Let me revisit the positive power of using technology to influence your children's spiritual lives. In the same way that I have learned to use my phone and other devices to share scripture, I do the same with prayer. A quick note to my kids reminding them that I am praying for them can provide them with just the encouragement they need to make it through the day. When I take a moment to let them know I just prayed about an upcoming test, or job interview, or even, a sticky relational situation, I am reminding them that God knows what they are facing and they aren't forgotten. Ephesians 5:16, reminds us to "make the most of every opportunity, because the days are evil." Our ever-present technology can help us to do just that!

DINNER & DISCIPLESHIP

I hope you know that I don't share these stories about my children to brag or to point out just how neat I think my children are... Trust me, we've had more than our share of failures! Rather, my goal is to encourage you that although "praying without ceasing" seems like a grown up idea, our children can incorporate this concept into their age and circumstances with a maturity that we would often not expect. Don't squelch their attempts at prayer, but instead use every opportunity to teach them when and how to pray. (Always and with great eagerness!!) Sometimes, our children have some quite surprising things to teach us about prayer. If you are open to learning from them as they demonstrate a childlike faith in bringing every part of their lives to their heavenly Father, your family will all grow closer to Him through the wonderful discipline of prayer.

90

www.characterhealth.com

FELLOWSHIP DEFINED: HELPING OUR CHILDREN TO DEVELOP GOD-HONORING FRIENDSHIPS

How exactly would you define the word "fellowship?" Is fellowship simply time spent with our friends or is there more to this concept? How we as parents define this term will very much determine the way we teach our children to look for and enjoy fellowship.

The Harper Collins Webster dictionary defines fellowship this way: association or counterpart of a like thing, fraternity or membership.

Consider this definition for a moment. Unlike mere acquaintanceship, fellowship embodies the notion of like-mindedness or of kindred spirit. This would be a relationship defined by a common goal, mindset, or belief system. So, as we clarify friendship and fellowship for our children, I believe that we need to differentiate between true fellowship with other like-minded believers and time spent with the unsaved or spiritually immature. One will help to build up our children and encourage their walk with the Lord; the other will naturally do just the opposite, unless we are very clear and purposeful in directing the time spent together. The Apostle Paul spoke clearly about this difference as we read in II Corinthians 6:14.

> *Do not be bound together with unbelievers;*
> *for what partnership have righteousness*
> *and lawlessness, or what fellowship has light*
> *with darkness?*

I do not want you to misunderstand me; I am certainly not saying that our children should never spend time with unsaved children. However,

I am saying that unless we are supervisory in those relationships, we run the risk of seeing our hard work of discipleship unravel before our eyes. All children take their friendships very seriously and I would contend that it is the rare child that can keep his or her heart "unbound" from an unbelieving friend. I will discuss many ways to have fruitful relationships with unsaved friends, relatives, and teammates throughout this section, but I believe we need to start with an understanding of what is true fellowship and what isn't true fellowship.

Who are your children's closest friends? Would you consider those children to be like-minded and characterized by making godly choices? Do you even know whom the children are that your children would define as their closest friends? As in so many other areas of our parenting, we cannot run the risk of losing our children's hearts because of laziness or negligence on our part. We should be keenly aware of not only who are children are spending time with, but how that time is being spent. Trust me, it isn't enough that our children assure us of the worthiness of a friendship. As children, they are not spiritually or emotionally mature enough to make wise and discerning decisions when it comes to choosing friends. Too often, what constitutes "beneficial" in a friendship to our children would be questionable and unacceptable to us. Take the time necessary to get to know the children your children spend time with and invest in building your own relationship with those children.

Children are children and no child will be a perfect friend for your child all of the time. However, there are friendships that are simply more beneficial than others. Just because our children prefer to spend time with certain other children is not necessarily an indicator that those children are the best friends for our children. Consider what the scripture tell us in I Corinthians 15:33:

Do not be deceived: "Bad company corrupts good morals."

If the majority of the time that your child spends with friends is in friendships where your child is the "good example," do not be shocked when you begin to see a corruption of their good morals. Although we do not want to judge our children's friends, we can certainly be fruit inspectors and evaluate carefully the good or bad fruit that is being produced by the friendship. Does your child always gravitate to children that would not fit the criteria of true fellowship? If this is the case, the fruit inspecting that needs to be done is most likely in your own home and with your own child's heart. Ask your own children good questions to discern what character qualities they are looking for in a friendship. Do those character qualities align with your family's standards and more importantly do they align with the Word of God? Sometimes, in our eagerness to make sure our children have many friends, we abandon our family standards or begin to make excessive compromises. Be careful! Compromising biblical standards will never result in friendships that bring honor and glory to God. Help your children learn to wait patiently and trust God to bring them sweet and God-honoring friendships.

Do your children find their closest friendships in your family? We have told our children from the very beginning that God placed them together in this family for a reason and therefore they needed to work hard to develop their sibling friendships. When their father and I are long gone, they will still have each other to turn to in friendship. Obviously, certain sibling pairings will more naturally gravitate to one another and that's a good thing. Teach your children to include everyone, but don't hesitate to cultivate those "special" sibling relationships.

The quality of the fellowship and friendships found within our homes should be one of our strongest testimonies for Christ. The world is filled with families who simply live together as roommates, or in more extreme cases, can't stand one another. Don't ignore or unconsciously promote sibling rivalry. Work hard to teach your children to love, serve, and pray for one another. Spend as much time as is necessary to teach your children how to quickly seek forgiveness and restore broken relationships with their siblings. Don't allow outside friendships to fill the void left by broken family relationships.

Sometimes, it will seem like certain children just can't learn to get along. In our own family, children number 2 and 3 spent much of their life competing with and annoying one another. We tried everything we knew to help those children get along. We encouraged them, exhorted them, and even punished them. Sometimes, I just wanted to knock their coconuts together, if you know what I mean... Despite our frustration with them, we still faithfully and continually prayed for them. When they left to attend the same college, we wondered how it would be with the battle taken to a new battlefield. We shouldn't have worried about it! God is always bigger than our worries and He took over and went to work in their lives. Through a series of unfortunate circumstances, Peter and Emma found themselves thrown together to walk through some difficult struggles. As they cared for one another with no other family to lean on, they began to grow closer. As they saw God work on their behalf, their hearts were bound together with an incredible bond. Now, as young married adults, there is no closer sibling pairing in our family. They love each other, pray for each other, and miss each other desperately now that they live far apart. Don't give up praying and interceding for your children. God is glorified through their family bond and He cares as deeply as you do about their sibling unity.

Truly good friends from outside of the family will never try to turn your children against their own brothers or sisters. Be very observant of how your children's friends treat your other children. If those friends are allowed to be unkind and disrespectful, it won't be long until you see that same fruit blossoming in the life of your own child. It takes time and involvement to see what is going on with your children and their friends; take the time! It is of vital importance! It is an unpleasant task, but when a friend is characteristically unkind to the other children in the family, it is time to intercede in the relationship. That's one reason it's so important to evaluate your children's friendships early in the relationship. Once our children have forged a strong bond with a friend outside the family, interceding for the good of your child and the other siblings will cause hurt and resentment. An alert parent sees the warning signs early and then acts for the good of the whole family.

Even with children that you would consider truly like-minded and that you feel are honestly one in fellowship with your children, you must still be alert and diligent. I personally don't believe that there is ever a need for closed bedroom doors when a friend is over visiting. Nothing good goes on behind closed doors and even trustworthy friends can get involved in conversations and actions with which we would not be pleased. Honestly, sometimes our own children are the initiators of those conversations and actions! If you announce that doors must remain open during visits and your own child reacts poorly to your decision, don't over-react. However, that's probably a good time to ask some clarifying questions. Seek to understand why your child feels the need to have a closed door, then, address any issues that arise.

Sometimes, our children feel as though they have to close their door to get away from the younger siblings. If that is the case, it is your cue to get on board and work on some younger child training. Out of respect for one another, our children should graciously allow their brothers and sisters some privacy with their friends. This would also be a great opportunity to teach our other children to be happy for the child that has the special friend visiting. In the same way we want our children to include their other siblings, we also want to teach the other children the important character quality of respect. In this case, respect shows itself as they graciously allow their brother or sister some privacy and special time with their friend.

Although I didn't force my children to include their younger siblings every time a friend was over, I did encourage them to consider their brother or sister's feelings. Especially when we had another family visiting for more than one day, I wanted the children to be inclusive, not exclusive with their friendships. Often, it was the visiting child whom was most considerate in including my other children and this served to heap coals on the unkind sibling's head! (Romans 12:20-21) Because we worked hard to teach our older children how to interact with younger children, and because we continually instructed our younger children in the important discipline of not annoying the older children needlessly, our mixed age groups played together very well. Their example provided an opportunity for their friends to enjoy the same sweet fellowship with children who weren't necessarily their peers.

Regardless of how like-minded or wholesome we might consider a friendship to be, ultimately we are still responsible to exercise a careful and watchful eye over all of our children's friendships. Just because a certain child comes from a family that we know well doesn't mean that we can just let the friendship proceed without evaluation. Consider these two admonitions from the Proverbs.

Proverbs 27:23 know well the condition of your flocks, and pay attention to your herds;

Clearly it is our responsibility to pay close attention to what is going on in our own children's hearts and friendships. Do you "know well" what is going on in your child's heart? If not... Why not? Take the time today to build a relationship of trust with your child so that you are able to discern or "pay attention," to what is going on in their life and heart. Notice that this verse does not exhort us to know well the condition of our best friend's flock, or our neighbor's flock, or the pastor's flock. We are to focus on the heart condition of our own children. I don't know about you, but that job is plenty big enough for me! I don't want the burden of worrying about anyone else's flock! That doesn't mean I can't evaluate the fruit that is evidenced in another child's actions and attitudes, but it does mean that "fixing" that other child is not my responsibility.

Speaking of our neighbor's flock... Occasionally, because of the unprofitable interactions between my children and a friend's children, I have had to limit or curtail my relationship with that friend. For many years, I tried to ignore the fruit of poor relationships between children, but after too many arguments and ugly interactions, I realized that just because I was close friends with another mother didn't mean that our children should necessarily become constant playmates. To be honest, I fought that decision in my heart. I felt ripped-off by the reality that because our children weren't positive playmates for one another, I had to limit our time together. Guess what? I just had to get over it! I realized that it wasn't that my kids were bad or my friend's kids were bad... They just weren't a good mix! Even as an adult, I know some women that I just don't mix well with and therefore, I don't spend much time with them. I certainly didn't give up on my women friends, but I reoriented my time spent with them. Instead of play dates with all of the children in tow, we began to meet for coffee after our husbands were home. Sometimes, I met with those women early in the morning before my children were even awake. Yes, it made logistics more difficult, but it solved the problem of unfruitful friendships that weren't bringing encouragement or uplifting our children. Don't let a desire for "woman time" derail your character training efforts!

Consider this second admonition, directed to mothers, from Proverbs 29-15:

> *But a child left to his own way brings shame to his mother.*

If a child left to his own way brings shame, I would assume that children left to their own way are equally shameful. Our children need our instruction and direction to learn how to make good decisions in how they spend their times of fellowship with like-minded friends. Before they go off to enjoy friend time, help them think through the activities in which they and their friends will be involved. Don't necessarily tell them what to do, but instead be available for suggestions as needed. We mothers spend the majority of time with our children. Don't squander that time by heedlessly ignoring the warning signs of a destructive friendship.

I would encourage you to be wise in the amount of time that your children spend with even the best of friends. Too much peer interaction will build appetites that we shouldn't encourage... appetites for constant activity and companionship outside of the family. Some alone and quiet time is so valuable for our children. It is during these times that their imaginations will be stretched and they will learn how to use their own time wisely without having to depend on others to fill their time for them. As well, I want my children to clearly learn how to hear the "still small voice of God." If every moment is filled with activity and friend-time, how will they ever learn to sit quietly and hear the voice of the Lord? Our children will push and sometimes manipulate us to ensure more friend time. Do not be easily swayed by their demands. Balance friend time with family time, individual time, rest, and service. Although your children may not thank you today, you will be building great habits for the future!

What about time with unsaved or worldly saved children? It is absolutely true that if you work hard to invest in your children's character, they will be in great demand by other parents. Be wise! Even if spending time with your child would seem to be helpful to someone else's child, there are certain relationships that just shouldn't be allowed. **You** be the guardian of your child's availability and don't allow another parent to use guilt or manipulation to pressure you into sacrificing your own child's wellbeing! Many times the other child is well aware of the reason that your child has been brought over to play and this can cause more harm than good. When our own children begin to recognize that they are being invited over as an example to others, they will be tempted to embrace pride and a self-righteous attitude. Who could blame them? If everyone held us up as the "good" example to follow, we'd be proud and self-righteous, too!

You should view your child's time with the unsaved or with immature believers as time on a mission field. However, DO NOT announce this fact to your child!!! Remember, even the most mature children will struggle with pride and arrogance if they see themselves as missionaries to all those other "needy" children. Instead, simply prepare your child to go visit with a heart of love and prepared to serve these children sacrificially.

We would never send an adult to a foreign mission field unaware of the dangers and pitfalls waiting for them. How much more seriously should we take the responsibility of sending our children into non-like-minded friendships to do battle for the Lord? We need to be aware of what goes on in the homes of those other children and if we do allow our children to go visit, we need to prepare them ahead of time for unwholesome traps to avoid. Such traps would include, but not be limited to: unrighteous entertainment, hostile parental relationships, alcohol in the home, use of bad language, etc. Don't sabotage your child and set them up to be taken by surprise and tripped up by any of these unacceptable behaviors. It takes humility to prepare our children without subtly teaching them that we are better than others. We often told our children, "Others may; we may not." It was never because we thought we were better or more righteous than another family. No, our standards were ours simply because they were the standards God had put before our family. We reminded our children that the Scheibner sin appetites might preclude certain activities for our family that could be totally acceptable for another family. Our job was never to judge others, but simply to be faithful to obey God in our own family and with our own family standards.

In my opinion, the best way to manage these non-like-minded friendships is for us to be engaged in any time spent together with these children. Yes, this means more work for you. This means having the children over to your home and being very aware of what is going on while they are there. While popping in and out to ensure that what is going on is acceptable is good, I would encourage you to go even further. Our goal for these young friends should be to see them come to a personal knowledge of and relationship with the Lord. With that end in mind, get to know these children well. You will be surprised at how eagerly even the toughest child will respond to an adult investing the time necessary to build a relationship with them. I have many friends that came from unsaved homes, but who came to know the Lord themselves after a friend's mom ministered love to them. It breaks my heart when I realize how many of my children's friends come from broken homes or homes that lack any type of strong family relationships. God has blessed our family and I consider it a privilege to love those kids with His love. I include many of these young people when I send out my scripture and prayer texts because after hours spent chatting over the kitchen counter they feel like my kids, too.

Be creative in finding ways to minister to these children. Perhaps once a week you could do a simple bible club with games, crafts, story-time and a snack. Your own children will love the opportunity to help set up and prepare a club for their friends. Be the cookie mom! Children will open up and share more than you would ever expect as they sit at your table and have cookies and milk. Sadly, many of the friends our children meet never have an opportunity to sit around the table at home and chat with their own mom or dad. Fewer and fewer children have intact families and the opportunity to be included in such a family will mean the world to these heart-hungry children! Food opens doors that seem to be nailed shut. Young men, especially, will talk for hours if the food keeps appearing. Find some simple snacks and keep them on hand for impromptu "kid-loving" sessions.

If your child is on a sports team or involved in a club or musical group, consider being the home where that team or group can gather. As you work to plan times of fun in your home, make the effort to involve other parents that you may not know. This is a great way to find out what is going on with the other children your child is building friendships with and it's also a way for you to begin to minister to the parents of these other children, as well. When you invite other parents to serve alongside you, you will be opening the door to new friendships and opportunities. If you have invested in filling your own spiritual cup, you will have the spiritual overflow you need to offer others-oriented ministry to the parents of your children's friends. Too often, these other adults feel isolated or friendless and opening our homes to their children will serve to open our homes to them, as well.

If it seems like the unsaved neighborhood kids are over **ALL** of the time, find a way to limit their visits without making them feel unwanted. Perhaps you could get a green flag and hang it outside your house when they are welcome to come over. Of course, then you have to actually put the flag out sometimes! I speak from experience, sadly. I'm naturally a quiet, introverted person, (Go figure... How did I end up with eight kids?) and sometimes, opening our home to other children just seemed like Too.Much.Work... I promise you, there is great blessing in opening your home! When I forced myself outside of my own comfort zone and opened our home in order to minister love to my children's friends, I was always blessed, encouraged, and bubbling over with ideas for the next time I could open my home to them. Having said that, there is nothing wrong with limiting the amount of time that your children spend with others. Don't allow a guilty conscience to cause you to be unwise in opening your home too often or for too long.

Make sure that you know how to lead a child to Christ! After you have invested in these children's lives, you don't want to be unprepared when they come to you desiring to begin a new relationship with Christ. We had many times that our children came to us after sharing the gospel with a friend and they needed an adult to help to lead the child in prayer. If you have a great deal of interaction with unsaved children, I would suggest having some inexpensive bibles and pre-printed "birth certificates" ready to fill out and present to the new Christian. These former "project" children may become the best like-minded fellowship that your child has ever known!

As your children share concerns with you about their unsaved or worldly friends, take those confidences seriously. Pray continually for your children's friends, both saved and unsaved. Be alert to changes in a friend's attitude, clothing choices, language, moods, etc. This isn't just so that we can protect our own children, but so that we can help these other dear children to avoid heading down roads of destruction with lifelong consequences. As parents, we have a great opportunity to provide a community of security where other young people know that if their own parents don't notice a problem in their lives, there are still adults aware of and concerned for them.

With this thought in mind, I would encourage you to build your own community of like-minded families with whom you can enjoy sweet fellowship. Not only will you be an example to your children, but you will also reap the benefit of other like-minded parents who will come alongside your children to encourage, exhort, and be available to offer counsel and protection. These friendships don't just happen, but must be cultivated and grown. Believe me, it is worth the effort! Sometimes "Mrs. Smith" can impart a truth to our children that we have been trying to help them to understand for weeks. Don't be discouraged that your child just couldn't seem to receive the lesson from you! Instead, thank God for like-minded friends that can help you in this parenting journey.

There is nothing sweeter than true like-minded fellowship. Encourage your children not to settle for friendship alone, but help them to develop a hunger for spiritual fellowship and friends with whom they can share their lives, laughter, and their Lord. Encourage them to build friendships based on spiritual goals and accountability. How sweet to see friends praying together, studying the word together, serving together, and memorizing scripture together!

Please don't underestimate the power and importance of friendship. Good friends can be an influence for good, encouraging growth and drawing our children back if they begin to go astray. Poor choices of friendship can do just the opposite, driving our children further away from our family, our standards, and God, Himself. Some families have tried to avoid the problem of ungodly friendships by isolating their children or by severely limiting their exposure to other young people. I absolutely believe there's a better way. Teach your children what to look for in friendship. Pray diligently on their behalf that God would provide sweet and uplifting friendships. Be a listening and non-judgmental ear when they come to you lonely, hurt, or isolated. Open your home to welcome others in and to facilitate friendships. Trust God to provide the friendships that will meet the needs of your child and teach them to serve others with an open heart and eager hands.

In our own family, we saw the immense value of God-honoring friendships firsthand. After my husband stepped down from the pulpit to begin our new ministry, we found ourselves living in our same small town, but needing to attend a new church. We knew that staying involved at the church he had planted would make the transition period much more difficult for the new pastor. Our options were limited! We finally found a like-minded church, but for our 15-year old daughter, there were no girls her age. Her old friends were busy at the old church and she found herself alone, lonely, and isolated. Her girl interactions were on the local swim team and she was the only Christian on the team. We watched her attitude toward us begin to change, then her actions, and finally, her heart. We ached as we watched our precious daughter slipping away. For her sake, we made the family decision to move away, even though we couldn't sell our home. We moved to another area and found a thriving church body. The young people in the church loved the Lord, loved serving, and quickly embraced our daughter. Within weeks we watched the light return to her eyes and the darkness fade away. Her new friends took their own walks with the Lord very seriously and they held her accountable to do the same.

I can't thank God enough for what He provided through those friendships. We were lavishing love on our daughter with all our hearts, but she was at a point in her life that she needed the security of not just family, but spiritual community, as well. Her God-honoring, self-sacrificing friends provided that security. They reached beyond their comfort zone to include and embrace the "new girl" and in the process they honored God. That's the kind of friends our children need. And, that's the kind of friends they must become if they too long to honor God through their friendships.

I cannot stress enough that just because someone claims the title of "Christian," does not mean that they believe and live by the same standards and convictions as your family. Four of my older children attended Christian college and with each subsequent student we saw more clearly how differently that word, "Christian," was defined. Quite honestly, it was always easier to explain the poor choices of a non-believing child or family, than the different standards of another Christian family. My children could understand and recognize that non-Christians had no reason to live by biblical standards. However, when another Christian family was living a life of poor choices and unbiblical standards, my children just walked away from those relationships confused. Too often, they began to doubt our family standards and wonder if we were just a little "too" spiritual. Be careful of the influence of Christians who don't adhere to biblical convictions!

Regardless of the sweetness of our children's friendships and times of fellowship, the truth is that all of these relationships involve two or more sinners interacting together. No friendship is without times of hurt feelings, misunderstood motives, or unkind actions. Because of this truth, it is very important to teach our children both how to forgive others and how to seek forgiveness themselves.

In our American culture, we have grown up saying the words, "I'm sorry." We use the same expression whether we simply misspell someone's name, step on his or her toe, or hit them with a brick in a moment of anger. "I'm sorry" is a nice concept, but it is incomplete. I picture "I'm sorry" as a band-aid placed over an oozing wound. Although the wound is covered, the infection is left to fester underneath. When the band-aid is removed by a repeated offense or a new injury, the infection is worse than ever. Seeking forgiveness is the ointment needed to solve the problem of infection caused by sin against one another.

Take the time to teach your children how to sincerely seek to be forgiven. This could begin with the words, "I'm sorry," but will go much further. Train your children to say the words, "will you forgive me?" Unlike simply apologizing, seeking forgiveness causes our children to admit their offense and to take ownership of that offense. Watch to see how much of a struggle it is for your children to articulate the words, "will you forgive me?" If they are unwilling to say these words, you need to teach into the pride that is holding them back. Pride will keep us from restoring relationships, simply because we refuse to humble ourselves and admit our guilt.

Along with the words, "will you forgive me," teach your children to insert the character quality or virtue that was violated by their actions. For example, "I'm sorry for calling you dummy, that was **unkind** of me." As your children think through the character quality that they are seeking forgiveness for violating, it will bring a deeper understanding of their own sin and need for forgiveness.

Along with seeking forgiveness, our children must learn to bring restoration to their wounded relationships. This may be as simple as giving back a grabbed toy or as elaborate as earning money to replace a broken keepsake. Help your children think through the restoration process and follow up to make sure that the situation has been resolved to everyone's satisfaction. Even when a friend or a friend's parents say, "That's ok, don't worry about it," encourage your child to follow through in the restoration process. Their offense is never simply between them and their friend. Rather, every offense involves God and out of obedience and reverence for Him the restoration process should be completed.

Seeking forgiveness isn't just for relationships outside of the family. Within our families we encounter many, many situations that require us to seek forgiveness and restoration. Asking for forgiveness from parents and siblings should be the norm, not saved for an extreme offense. We parents can do the most effective training in this area by modeling the forgiveness and restoration model ourselves. When we wrong our children, we should be quick to seek their forgiveness and then to find appropriate ways to restore with them. Fortunately, our children are always so quick to forgive us with hearts that long to restore. Seeing Mom and Dad seeking forgiveness with one another will go far in teaching this important concept to our children. Learning to seek forgiveness within the home will empower our children to quickly seek forgiveness and initiate restoration outside of the home.

Sometimes children will latch onto the words "will you forgive me" and want to use them as an escape clause. If your child is quickly blurting out the words, or saying them over and over, but you don't see any godly sorrow, or doubt true repentance, slow the process down. Many times I have sent my children to another room to consider not just what they needed to say, but what attitude needed to be in their heart. Just mouthing the words, "will you forgive me," is not the solution to interpersonal problems. Only seeking forgiveness and restoration from sincere motives can bring healing to a hurting relationship.

At other times, our children will be the one's who have been wounded. We must teach them to extend forgiveness without a spirit of retaliation. The model is found in Luke 17: 3-4 where Jesus gives us instruction about how to train our hearts to forgive.

> *Be on your guard! If your brother sins, rebuke him: and if he repents forgive him. And if he sins against you seven times a day, and returns to you seven times, saying, 'I repent,' forgive him.*

Our children must learn to forgive others, whether it be a brother or sister or parent, or friend, regardless of whether that person sins against them again, or not. Teach your children to be generous with their forgiveness. This does not mean, however, that our children must spend time with children that consistently hurt them or have a blatant disregard for their feelings and possessions. Help your child to be discerning in deciding when it is necessary to end an unfruitful friendship.

We should model for our children an abundant spirit in regards to both seeking forgiveness and forgiving others. It costs us nothing but our pride to humble ourselves and seek forgiveness. Forgiveness and restoration must be an integral part of your home. Children who know what it means to be forgiven at home will be much more likely to seek forgiveness outside of their homes. Regardless of how your children's friends respond to their overtures of seeking forgiveness and restoration, it is still the right thing to do. As your children consistently seek to make their relationships whole, they will enjoy great fruit and success in their friendships and their opportunities to witness for Jesus will be strengthened.

True friendships and fellowship take work. Teach your children to be loyal and caring friends. There are times when they will be mistreated by others, but you can help them to use those opportunities to cement in their own hearts what kind of friend God would desire for them to be to others. The hard work is worth it. Be involved with your children's friends, both saved and unsaved, the fruit will be priceless in your children's lives.

"True friendships and fellowship take work. Teach your children to be loyal and caring friends."

SCRIPTURE MEMORIZATION: EQUIPPING OUR CHILDREN TO STAND

Psalm 119:11- *I have hidden Your word in my heart that I might not sin against You.*

Psalm 119:16-*I shall delight in Thy statutes; I shall not forget Thy word.*

Psalm 119:34-*Give me understanding that I may observe Thy law, And keep it with all my heart.*

Psalm 119:109-*My life is continually in my hand, Yet I do not forget Thy law.*

The memorized word of God, abiding in our children's hearts, is a safeguard against sin, a stronghold of protection, and a shelter in times of storm. I can think of no more important discipline to help prepare our children to stand in evil times than scripture studied, memorized, and permanently implanted in their hearts and lives. I can think of no more important discipline in *our* lives than scripture studied, memorized, and permanently implanted in our own hearts and lives!

I can't say it any more clearly. Memorizing the word of God is imperative for anyone desiring to live a godly Christian life. But, having said that, how do we get there from here? Scripture memorization is hard work. It takes diligence, determination, repetition, patience, and prayer! But, with all this effort comes great fruit. An understanding of the importance of scripture memorization is one of those truths in which more is caught, than taught. You can tell your children over and over how important it is to hide God's word in their hearts, but unless they see you committed to memorizing His word for yourself, they will lack the conviction necessary to commit to this discipline wholeheartedly.

If you have never memorized scripture yourself, don't lose heart. Just begin the practice of memorizing with your children. Don't be discouraged by how much easier the task is for them than for you...they have young fertile brains, unlike our older tireder noggins! I would suggest starting simply. Pick a favorite verse to begin and write it out word for word on a 3x5 card. Carry that card with you wherever you go and review the verse over and over. Make sure you memorize your scripture exactly as it is written and work hard to be disciplined in this area. When we just memorize the "gist" of the verse we run the risk of missing the context or full meaning of the verse. Have your children quiz you and you do the same for them. Soon you will all have your first verse memorized and you will have built confidence for both you and your children that this is a task that can be accomplished.

May I encourage you to require everyone to take the extra effort and memorize the reference as well as the verse? The Word of God is far more effective than our own words when we are counseling, teaching, or simply sharing with others. I can tell you from experience that it's very frustrating when I have to say, "There's a verses somewhere in the bible that says..." Work hard and memorize those references to increase the influence that God's Word will have in the lives of others!

The first verse that I taught all of my children was Ephesians 6:1.

> *Children obey your parents in the Lord, for this is right.*

This verse was so foundational to all of the character qualities that I was trying to teach my children. Throughout the day, we found many opportunities for them to repeat that verse to me... over and over. One of my friends shared this story about teaching her son this verse. He would freeze every time she asked him to recite the verse and just repeat, "Children, obey, obey, OBEY!" He had the right idea, but that wasn't quite the goal. She just kept encouraging him and soon he knew the verse word perfect.

When my oldest children were very young, I began to teach them parts of verses to introduce them to the idea of memorization and the importance of knowing God's word. Here are the simple statements we memorized. I am including the reference verse that each statement is based upon, so that you can look up the entire verse in its context. As my children memorized these shortened parts of complete verses, I was able to use what they had memorized in our teaching times. For example, as I was talking to them about their need for salvation, each of my children wanted to believe that they were not sinners. The very first memorization answered that question and they soon realized that God's Word stated clearly, "All have sinned." In a like manner, when we were praying for God to supply something we needed, the reminder that "My God shall supply all your needs," helped them to be patient and wait on the Lord. Every day, more practical applications of what they had memorized became clearer to all of us. Remember, simply memorizing the Word of God is of little benefit to our children. It is as we put that memorized Word into action that we will see growth and Christ-centered change in our homes. As your children get older, be slow to tell them exactly how to apply the Word to their lives. Instead, ask them good questions so that they can discern the application on their own. As they learn how to take what they have memorized and make it applicable to their own lives, they will learn to take ownership of their own walk with the Lord. That ownership is the ultimate goal of our teaching and the foundation of a personal relationship with the Lord that will anchor our children's hearts in times of storm and blessing.

Be gentle and gracious as you begin the process of teaching your children how to memorize the scriptures. Reward them for verses that are well memorized and encourage and exhort your children to give scripture memorization their best efforts. Do not turn memorization into something to be punished. Too often, I found myself scolding my children the hour before our Awana club because they didn't know their verse. The only thing my scolding accomplished was a nervous child, who crammed a verse into their short-term memory in order to appease my anger. Definitely not one of my best "mommy moments" and not the way I want my children to look at scripture memorization. The Word of God should never be seen as punishment or as something that produces guilt. Conviction...Yes, but guilt...Never!

Simple starter memory work:

A is for All: All have sinned (Romans 3:23)

B is for Believe: Believe in the Lord Jesus Christ and you will be saved (Acts 16:31)

C is for Christ: Christ died for us (Romans 5:8)

D is for Devote: Devote yourselves to prayer (Colossians 4:2)

E is for Every: Every good and perfect gift is from above (James 1:17)

F is for Follow: Follow me and I will make you fishers of men (Matt. 4:19)

G is for God: God opposes the proud (James 4:6)

H is for He: He is not here for He has risen as He said (Matthew 28:6)

I is for I: I am crucified with Christ, therefore I no longer live (Gal. 2:20)

J is for Jesus: Jesus died and rose again (I Thessalonians 4:14)

K is for Keep: Keep the way of the Lord (Genesis 18:19)

L is for Love: Love the Lord your God (Deuteronomy 6:5)

M is for My: My God shall supply all your needs (Philippians 4:19)

N is for Not: Not by works of righteousness (Titus 3:5)

O is for Open: Open my eyes (Psalm 119:18)

P is for Pray: Pray without ceasing
(I Thessalonians 5:17)

Q is for Quick: Be quick to hear and slow to
speak (James 1:19)

R is for Run: Run and tell His disciples
(Matthew 28:7)

S is for Salvation: Salvation is from the Lord
(Jonah 2:9)

T is for Trust: Trust in the Lord with all your heart
(Proverbs 3:5)

U is for Unless: Unless the Lord builds the house
they labor in vain (Psalm 127:1)

V is for Vindicate: Vindicate me Lord (Psalm 7:8)

W is for Where: Where is your sting, Oh death? (I Corinthians 15:55)

X is for (E)Xamine: Examine yourselves (II Corinthians 13:5)

Y is for Yield: Yield now and be at peace (Job 22:21)

Z is for Zaccheus: Zaccheus, you come down! (Luke 19:5)

These were the verses and statements that worked best for us. You may have other verses that would be important to incorporate for your family. After the children had memorized these short statements, the transition to whole verses was not difficult at all. When I used these verses in training my children, the shortness of the verse was helpful since they could understand what I was teaching them without getting lost in a lengthy portion of scripture.

There are some other verses that I insisted that all of my children memorize. These included the Romans Road, (Romans 3:23, 5:28, 6:23, 8:1 and 12:1-2) Psalm 23, the fruit of the spirit found in Galatians 5, and I Corinthians 13. Together we memorized Philippians 4 and Psalm 119. Because I felt that these verses were so foundational to their Christian growth, we didn't just memorize the verses and move on. Instead, I tried to use the verses, repeat the verses, and refer back to them often to keep them at the forefront of our teaching.

We have always had our children involved in church programs and those programs all required scripture memorization. The children earned many ribbons and trophies in these programs, but I felt that it was also important that they build the habit of scripture memorization without the need for outside rewards. Memorizing together as a family helped to build the habit and the reward was a strong sense of family accomplishment. This is not to say that we never gave tangible rewards for family scripture memorization. Sticker charts gave us a way to track scripture memory goals and as goals were met, we found various ways to celebrate those successes. Sometimes we would set out a specific, much desired reward for a goal met in memorizing a longer piece of scripture. Tailor the goals and rewards to the personalities of your own children for the greatest impact.

While the older hymns of the faith are a wonderful addition to your bible training times, praise songs and scripture songs are an equally helpful aid to your scripture memory toolbox. So many of these songs are simply the words of scripture set to an easily remembered tune. For some of your children, using music to assist in memorization will make the difference between frustration and success. There are many CD's available to assist you in teaching these songs to your children.

ese valuable resources.

al verses, I think it is very

ve our children memorize the

are most pertinent to their lives at

ment. For example, when one of my

dren was struggling with lying, she spent many weeks memorizing all of the scriptures pertaining to lying and dishonesty. Soon she had a clear understanding of how God felt about a lying tongue and exactly what He had to say about deceit. Those verses, hidden in her heart, began to convict her and change her attitude about truthfulness in a way that my continual reminders (nagging) could not. When another child was struggling with discouragement, we looked up many joy verses and he committed those to memory. What a safeguard to have scriptural truth to replace Satan's lies as he struggled to find joy in his circumstances.

Take the time to help your children consider what verses would be the most helpful to them. As they share fears they are struggling with, doubts about various issues, or as you see sin appetites taking root in their lives; keep a record of these topics. Use a concordance to look up verses that apply to each need and then have your children write them out, word for word, on index cards. As they memorize these verses, you are equipping them to do serious battle with the sin appetites and areas of weakness in their young lives.

Use vacations or school breaks to work on larger family scripture memorization projects. There is something wonderful about memorizing an entire book of the bible together. Although it can seem a daunting challenge, there is a great sense of family success and victory when the book is completed. If you don't feel that your children are ready for that big of a challenge yet, memorize a book of the bible yourself, as an example to them. As you practice your memorized verses out loud with your children, you will be building an anticipation in their hearts for the time when they are finally going to be ready to memorize an entire book with you. Rejoice when your children are tough on you and demand that you repeat your memorized verses "Word Perfectly." They're outwardly demonstrating the standard you've been impressing on their hearts and besides, it's good for you!

When my husband was serving as the pastor of our church in Maine, he set out a scripture memorization goal each summer. He chose a portion of scripture, a psalm, or an entire book of the bible and challenged the church families to complete their memorization by August 30th. On the last Sunday of August, our Sunday evening service simply consisted of families sharing aloud the scripture they had memorized all summer. That service was one of my favorite times of the year. The summer challenge provided a great way to encourage the families in the church, and what an impetus it was for the families who hadn't participated in the challenge to jump on board and participate the next summer.

As an encouragement, when I was going through a particularly difficult time in my life, I purposed to memorize the entire book of James. I had never memorized an entire book before and honestly, I wasn't sure that I could do it. As I patiently plugged away at committing the book to memory, God used those verses to still my troubled thoughts and redirect my anxious worries to the truth reflected in His Word. How I long for my children to be able to find that same peace! What a precious gift we give our children when we teach them the life-changing skill of hiding the Word of God in their hearts.

Service: Helping Our Children Learn To Put Their Faith Into Action

Service is the action that takes head knowledge and turns it into heart knowledge in our children's lives. As one of my children would say, "service is faith with skin on it." Without the outlet of service, our children are no better than the Pharisees, men who knew the right answers but didn't live out the concepts in their own lives. Fortunately for us, service is such an easy concept to teach our children, IF we are willing to be servants ourselves!

Where does service begin? I believe that our children need to learn to serve faithfully and cheerfully at home first, before they begin to practice service on a regular basis outside of the home. Allowing our children to perform all of their service outside of the home, with no heart to serve in the home is poor training for life, where much of the service we perform is in our own homes. The exception to this rule would be service done together as a family unit.

When we participate in service to others, we are living out the teaching found in Mark 12, to love our neighbors as ourselves. Service can be as simple as the offer of a glass of water or as elaborate as opening our homes to the homeless, and it runs the gamut in between. No child is too young and no adult is to old to serve, and service to others should be the hallmark of the believer.

Did you catch what I just said... No child is too young to serve? How in the world can a baby serve? When I was a young mom, an older mom challenged me to be generous in allowing other people to hold my baby. She explained to me that for a lonely or elderly person, the privilege of holding a tiny baby filled a heart need that often went unmet. Once I learned this concept, I was more than eager to allow my little baby to "serve" in this way. Of course, I was blessed as well, as my baby learned to trust me and to have confidence that I would never hand her to someone that would bring harm to her. Moms, trust me you can hand your baby to someone else and they will be just fine! Obviously, we must practice discernment as we hand our babies off, but there is no reason to fear doing so. When we are certain that only we can be trusted with our baby, we reap the fruit of clingy, whiny children who are fearful of others. Be wise, but also be generous with sharing the blessing your baby can be to another person.

Babies can also serve as great conversation initiators. Often, as I was out with my child, I would be able to strike up a conversation with another mother and her child. Talking about our children built an immediate bridge of communication and understanding and I was able to start some wonderful relationships this way. What a relief it was to realize that many of the questions I had and situations I was encountering as a young mom were common to all young moms! So I repeat, no child is too young to serve!

Serving others is at the very core, simply considering the needs of others as more important than our own needs. We'll begin by examining the many ways that our children can serve at home and how to train them in those service opportunities. In the beginning, our children will need us to point out the many service opportunities that surround them, but ultimately our goal should be that recognizing and embracing needs and service opportunities on their own is what characterizes our children. As in all other areas of their spiritual lives, we want our children to take ownership of their serving and service opportunities. I definitely don't want to become the mother of a twenty-something who finds herself saying, "Go open that door! Can't you see her hands are full?" Our children won't just morph into servants, they must be taught as we model and walk together with them through service opportunity after service opportunity.

We should be seeking to develop young adults who are *eage*r to serve, not just simply *willing* to serve. Let me illustrate the difference between these two heart attitudes. If you break your leg and I call you and say, "If you need anything, give me a call," I am a willing servant. Whatever need you have, I will be willing to fill it, but I am waiting for you to let me know what you need. There is nothing intrinsically wrong with this attitude, however I think the Lord is looking for something more from those who are His. Let's look at the same situation from the attitude of someone with an eager heart. I would call you after hearing the bad news about your broken leg and say something like this, "I'm so sorry to hear about your leg. I'm bringing over a casserole this afternoon that you can eat tonight or throw in the freezer. I thought I could give your bathrooms a quick scrub while I'm there and if there is anything else you need to have done, just write it down before I arrive so that we don't miss anything." Do you see the difference? One response requires the needy person to seek you out for help; the other response looks ahead and sees needs that can be filled immediately. This is the attitude we want to inspire in our children, an attitude of eagerness, not willingness.

Do you have an eager servant's heart, a willing servant's heart, or actually, any type of heart to serve? Your children will learn their excitement for serving as they observe you eagerly looking for and taking advantage of opportunities to serve others. Be careful though, as moms it is sometimes easier to serve outside of our homes, rather than simply serving at home. I must be honest and admit that there have been times that my children ate peanut butter and jelly for dinner while I was preparing a lovely three-course meal for someone else. That is *not* the testimony of service that I want to impart to my children. Yes, I want them to learn to esteem others more highly than themselves, but I do not want them to grow up believing that serving them is somehow less important to me and of less value to God than serving others.

I've often pondered why it's so much easier to serve outside my home, rather than inside it's four walls. The conclusion I've come to isn't very pretty and it's based in a wrong heart attitude. Simply put, I believe outside service affords us more opportunities for praise from others. It doesn't matter how small my service to others actually is; I can always count on enthusiastic thanks and effusive praise from those I serve. However, when I perform the same small service in my home, oftentimes my service is overlooked or unappreciated. After all, I'm mom... I'm just supposed to do those things! Yes, my family needs to learn to be thankful, but that's a different issue. My responsibility is to serve joyfully regardless of what anyone else does or says. Learning to serve joyfully at home has forced me to consider whom my service is ultimately intended to please. If I am looking to please and be praised by my family members, too many times I'll be disappointed. But, when I am serving simply because I love the Lord and I'm thankful for the service opportunities He's provided for me through caring for my family, I will be blessed. I'm not always successful at keeping that type of service as my goal, but I'm learning every day how better to bless my family by loving God and serving them. The more I can model that type of attitude, the easier it will be for my children to adopt that same attitude in their service. I never want to be a bad example for them; so serving from a right heart attitude is an ever-present goal in my life.

Begin teaching your children to serve at home by asking them good open-ended questions. "How can we serve your dad today?" or "What could we do that would be a service to your big sister?" Don't answer the question right away for your child if they hesitate in their response. Allow them to think and consider service opportunities for themselves. After awhile, if they really are stumped for what to do, offer them some choices of services they could perform.

Here is a list of some simple service opportunities to get you started.

1. Make someone's bed for him or her.
2. Complete a chore for a particularly busy older sibling.

3. Bring a hard-studying sibling a treat.
4. Write a note of encouragement.
5. Clean someone's room.
6. Clean out the car.
7. Carry someone else's laundry to their room.
8. Keep the baby occupied while mom fixes dinner.
9. Etc.

A way of serving that we encouraged in our home was service through "preferring" a brother or sister. Preferring looks slightly different than straight out service. Preferring involves giving up something that we have a perceived "right" to claim, for the benefit of someone else. For example, when it was one child's turn to sit in the front seat of the car (a much loved privilege in our home,) they could serve, or prefer, a sibling by extending that privilege to the other child. The beauty of preferring is in the recognized sacrifice of one child for the wellbeing of another. Preferring reaches deep into the heart of the child and established their willingness to give sacrificially when such a sacrifice is not "technically" required. To be honest, preferring is harder than just serving. It's easy to serve or give something that costs me nothing. Preferring requires sacrifice and sometimes sacrifice is hard!

Interestingly, I have observed that children who have been consistently trained to serve their brothers and sisters will be eager to find ways to serve their parents, as well. We never specifically taught our children to serve us, but they transferred the teaching to serve others into creative ways to serve mom and dad as well. What a blessing this service was at the times when I was ill or I was kept busy caring for other sick children, as the "serving" child filled the gaps and kept me from falling far behind in my household duties.

The illness of a brother or sister is a great opportunity for your children to learn to serve. As they watched me prepare a cozy room for a sick child, my children were learning the invaluable skill of making a place of comfort for the suffering. Teach your children what it takes to make a sickroom cozy and inviting. When I had a feverish child, I would tidy the sickroom and exchange the dirty sheets with fresh clean sheets taken straight from the dryer. It only takes a few moments in the dryer to make sheets soft and warm and the comfort they impart to a sick child is well worth any effort. I showed the children how to mix juice and ginger ale to make a cool drink to fill the need for pushing fluids. I often asked the other children to pick out some age-appropriate books to place next to the bed or to set up a CD player and some good story CD's. Ask your children; they will have great ideas about what would be enjoyable for a child confined to bed. Now, as I am driving home from a Dr.'s visit with a sick child, I can just call ahead and the children go into action to prepare a comfortable room for their sick sibling. Naturally, caring for a sick sibling came more easily to some of my children than others, however, I still worked hard to teach each of them how to be others-oriented and compassionate toward a hurting sibling. As they learned this valuable skill of caring for their brothers and sisters, they were building habits and skills for a lifetime.

Take the time to build the habit of service at home. Often, we want to rush our children into public service. Sometimes, I wonder if perhaps this rush to have them serve publicly is for their good or our own pride. Be patient in building the foundation of a servant's heart at home, where sometimes our good deeds go unnoticed, and you will have gone far in preparing your children to serve outside the home with a heart motivated by love, not a desire for recognition.

Trust me, if you take the valuable time necessary to train children whom are known for their servant hearts, there will be no lack of opportunities for your children to serve outside the home. The difficulty will come in making the decision of which service opportunities are appropriate and beneficial for your children. I learned from hard experience that there were some people who just felt that they deserved to be served. Because my children had a reputation of serving others the expectation became that they were obligated to serve everyone at all times and at all costs. Be careful that your children aren't embittered or wounded by ungrateful people who take advantage of their servant attitudes. Sadly, we will all run into those types of folks... Takers, who have no thought for anyone but themselves. Help your children learn to be forgiving when they are wrongfully used, but keep the avenues of communication open between them and you so that you can help them extricate themselves from those situations and people.

There are innumerable opportunities for our children to serve in our churches and communities. Service in their own church is what will transform our children's attitude toward church from "the church," to "my church." All children, even the youngest, should have some avenue of service in their church. Yes, this may take some work and commitment on your part, but the fruit will be so sweet. Even if your church has paid cleaning help, there are still many projects that get overlooked or neglected. Your children will feel that they are an important and necessary part of the smooth running of their church as they find jobs to complete and needs to fill that are theirs alone. At different times, we have completed all or some of these projects for our church: cleaning and sanitizing the nursery toys, deep cleaning the bathrooms, cleaning out the refrigerator, weeding the church flower beds, trimming the shrubbery, vacuuming the seats in the sanctuary, washing the nursery crib bedding, filling envelopes for mailings, delivering meals to new moms, and more. If you wonder what jobs need to be done, simply contact your church office and tell them that you and your children are looking for a way to serve. As you serve alongside your children, you will have opportunities to teach them diligence, faithfulness, and a finisher's attitude. Take the time to teach your children to not simply get the service done, but to do all of their service with the goal of excellence. I have never met a pastor or church staff member who wasn't absolutely delighted to have one of the church families serving by filling the all to present needs of the church. Believe me, you won't be a burden by asking what needs to get done... You're family will be a blessing!

I must add some background information here. For ten years, my husband was the pastor of a church plant. As church planters, we did anything and everything to ensure the smooth running of the ministry. **But,** that wasn't when we began serving in our local church. Long before Steve ever graduated from seminary and began the church, we had already put in countless hours filling the needs of the body. Before we even had children, Steve and I were committed to serving wherever and whenever we were needed. Because we had such a deep commitment to serving, it was just natural to bring our children alongside of us and to get them busy and engaged in the nitty-gritty work of the church. Along the way, we began to clearly see the benefit of that commitment to service as its fruit blossomed in our children's lives. We never had to "force" our children to attend church. Because of their service in the church they felt a deep attachment to the church. We never sensed that we were bringing our children along with us to the church; rather, it was our family journeying together to our church. I'm convinced service is what made the difference. Even today, as members of a large church, our children just naturally find ways to serve and the staff members know that when there is a need, we are a family they can call upon.

If you are a part of a ministry family, I would say that this attitude of service in the church is particularly necessary. It is easy to feel that we serve enough because dad is on staff, but this is not the attitude that we want to build into our children's lives. Those children who feel that they are the exception to the rule, that because of their parent's position they don't need to serve in the church, are the same children who will have the propensity to become "PK's;" children who are looking to be served and feel entitled to special privileges or recognition. As soon as possible, help your children to recognize that they are an important part of the ministry, by finding a specific area in which they can be committed to serving. It's vitally important that we remind our children that we are nothing special as a ministry family. In fact, we are extra blessed when we are called upon to serve the Lord... Service is a privilege when you are asked to serve the Lord of the Universe!

Please allow me to share just a word about heart attitudes to be aware of as our children begin to serve others. Unfortunately, many of these attitudes are simply reflections of our own attitudes toward serving, so check your own heart first before you reprimand your children! If you recognize that your own heart attitude needs to change, seek the Lord's forgiveness, take the necessary steps to change your attitude, then proceed to train your children. Also, if you see attitudes in your children and recognize them as a reflection of your own poor attitudes, take the time to seek your children's forgiveness for your poor example. Be transparent and let them know that God has been working in your heart and that you are committed to changing your attitude and helping them as they change their attitudes also. Some children will begin to view themselves as overworked victims, forced to serve because, "Someone has to do it..." Be on the alert for this attitude!! Our service should flow from a heart full of gratitude to the Lord Jesus Christ for what He has done for us, not from a "poor me," attitude of self-pity. What should we do if we see such an attitude developing in our children? Simply telling them that they need to serve out of a grateful heart will not accomplish anything. Rather, the more time we spend in the Word, reminding our children of the love and sacrifice that was poured out for them on the cross by Jesus, the more they will love and be grateful to Him. My husband has repeatedly said this about his own life, "After what He's done for me, what wouldn't I be willing to do for Him?" Seeing this attitude exhibited in their father's life has had a huge testimony and impact on our children's attitude toward service.

Another attitude to be aware of in our children's life is the attitude of pride that can develop because of their service. When we begin to see our children exhibiting an attitude of, "This place is sure lucky to have me!" immediate action is required. Again, this is a misunderstanding of the attitude of gratitude that we should have toward Jesus Christ. Allowing us to serve Him by serving others is a gracious blessing from the Lord! Without an avenue to show our gratitude toward Him through service, we would be frustrated by our inability to show our thankfulness in a tangible way. God doesn't "need" us because of our special abilities or talents, He chooses to allow us to serve Him, through our service to others, simply because He loves us! Even at home, those same attitudes can surface, especially in older children who feel like the family is "lucky" to have them and their stellar example. Pride is so insidious and we do our children no favors when we leave it go unchecked.

So then, what is the correct response to this attitude of pride we may sometimes see in our children's hearts? Again, the more time we spend showing them the enormity of Christ's love for them, the more they will grow in a grateful attitude of thanksgiving. However, I wouldn't stop there. For a time, I would not allow the children the privilege of serving. When serving becomes a "right" our children do not have the same humility as when service for the Lord is a privilege. When you see your children growing closer to the Lord, in gratitude, then you can re-institute service opportunities and your children will embrace them with a thankful heart. The same consequence will be just as effective in your home. When they are held back from serving and, oh by the way, the extra privileges and grown-up benefits that come from serving responsibly, suddenly service to others will become a much-desired privilege. It's a funny truth about children... Once they can't have something it becomes the one thing they want! As you look for opportunities for your children to serve within the church, be aware of your children's areas of giftedness, but do not be limited by only encouraging them to serve in those areas. All of the Scheibner children were born loving to be behind a microphone. We had to teach them to love holding a plunger as much as they loved to hold a microphone! For them, it was no challenge at all to sing a solo, play an instrument, or publicly read the scripture. To allow them to choose only to serve in those areas would have been a grave disservice to my children and would have limited their availability to the Lord. As they scrubbed toilets, stuffed envelopes, and washed dishes, my children were actively building their eternal resumes! As the wife of a pastor, I was dismayed to see too many folks with "specialist" attitudes. People wanted to serve in the areas they enjoyed and that's great, but there are so many unglamorous, undignified, uninteresting jobs that must be taken care of for a church to run smoothly. Those jobs were hard to assign, and often, the most over-worked folks in the church found themselves doing even more because *someone* needed to get the job done! Isn't that true in our homes, as well? Remember, just because a child enjoys doing certain jobs more than others doesn't mean that they should always get the job of their choice. It takes work and a careful consideration of what's going on behind the scenes, but a diligent mom will make sure that the workload is distributed fairly and equitably.

If, as the old saying goes, idle hands are the devil's workshop, consistent service in the church will develop children who don't have spiritually idle hands. Those folks in the church who don't discipline themselves to stay busy serving, are too often the same people who find themselves trapped in cycles of gossip and discontent. If you keep busy serving, you won't have time to waste in unprofitable activities and neither will your children. If you or your children find yourself discontent or grumbling about your church, may I encourage you to get even busier finding ways to serve and bless the body? As you serve, your love and commitment to your church will grow and you'll find discontent replaced by gratitude and a loving heart.

The non-church community also offers many opportunities for service that our children can fill. I would encourage you to be available to serve alongside your children as they venture into the world of community service. My children have been challenged as they served meals to the homeless on Thanksgiving and Easter or delivered packages of food, toys, and clothing for the Christmas Angel Tree. Seeing the lack of simple necessities in the lives of these people caused my children to appreciate more the blessings that God and their hard-working father had generously provided for them.

A wonderful yearly ministry that can involve your whole family is Operation Christmas Child run by Samaritan's Purse ministries. This great ministry delivers shoe boxes packed with age appropriate toys, hygiene supplies, school supplies, and more to needy children around the world. Filling shoeboxes provides a wonderful opportunity to invite other children and their families into your home to serve together. When service is coupled with fellowship; friendships blossom and needy children will be blessed.

When I was growing up, I had little or no interaction with the elderly. As a consequence of this, I really struggled with fears as a young adult trying to minister effectively to older folks. When my own elderly parents were dying, I made a promise to myself that my children would not have the same reticence to serving these dear people, simply because they had never been exposed to them. As a result of this promise, I found a nursing home where my children could serve on a consistent basis. As they read books aloud to the elderly men and women and played games of bingo and go fish with them, my children grew to love and appreciate these dear folks. The stories that the older people were so willing to share with my children gave them a deeper understanding of earlier times and the struggles that some of these folks had survived. The blessing to my children and myself far outweighed any service that we were able to offer.

I mentioned earlier, that service affords us the opportunity to teach our children diligence, faithfulness, and a finisher's attitude. Do not take these learning opportunities for granted. Many times, our children will begin a new service opportunity with excitement and great resolve, but as the service becomes difficult, demanding, or just plain boring, our children may begin to lose interest and their commitment to serve will wane. Do not miss the teaching moment that your children are presenting to you! Insist that they continue to serve diligently and faithfully. Not all service projects need to be continued indefinitely, but choose an ending point that is beneficial to everyone concerned. DO NOT allow your children to quit just because they are no longer excited about that particular service. Teach them to finish whole-heartedly the service that they have begun. This is a tremendous life lesson that will serve them well, long after they have left your home.

One final thought about service... The deepest friendships our children will build are forged as they serve alongside one another. For dating couples, serving together will present a clear picture into one another's heart. True services takes away the need for "advertising" in the dating process, as couples turn their attention and energy away from one another, and instead, pour their efforts into serving and blessing others. Too often, when our times with friends are simply spent "hanging out" or just chatting, we stray into conversations and actions that are non-productive and sometimes, even regrettable. Serving together always seems to change that dynamic. I've been amazed at the things I've learned from "shy" people who were serving beside me. Service opens up avenues of communication and cements relationships building the trust necessary to share freely with one another.

Opportunities to serve abound! As you begin to look for ways to serve, often the problem becomes choosing which service is best suited to you and your children. We can't fill every need, but as you seek the Lord in prayer, He will be faithful to show you where you can best be used. Then, as you confidently take advantage of all of these opportunities, the important lessons that you have taught your children about the Word, prayer, fellowship, and scripture memorization, will come to life and transform your children, your family, your church, and your community through service.

A Final Word to Mothers

In the past four years, since the initial publication of Dinner and Discipleship, I've had the opportunity to travel all over the United States, as well as overseas, to teach moms the important discipline of mentoring and discipling their children. I've met and been blessed by such incredible women. So many of the women I've been privileged to meet want the best for their children and their families, but they want so much more. Women, all over the world, want to be influencers for Christ. They want to raise children who will impact the world for Christ, but they want to fill that role themselves, also.

I think God put that desire in our hearts. Like the early disciples, His desire is that His people would be training others to love Him, worship Him, serve Him, and share Him with others. Being wives and moms doesn't exempt us from that task, and in fact, it perhaps equips us uniquely to make an incredible difference in the lives of others.

Each time I teach these principles of discipleship, I begin my talk by forewarning my audience that I will have a requirement for them at the end of the session. Now, I'd like to place that requirement on you, as well. By the end of my teaching, I tell the listeners that I want them to have already begun to think about whom, outside their home, they will begin to disciple. For some, that decision is easy and they leave the session raring to go! For others, it takes more time and some focused prayer, but I admonish them to choose someone and make it happen.

I want you to make that commitment today! Whom will you begin to pour yourself into as you share the truths of God's Word? I think we all desire to be agents of change for the Kingdom of God, but unless we make a specific plan, that just won't happen. Some of you may think you're too young in the faith to disciple another believer. May I challenge you on that idea? Everyone, and I mean everyone, has someone younger than they are in the faith. Maturity as a believer doesn't always equal maturity in physical age! Just because you are young doesn't mean that you can't be used to share what it means to walk in faithful relationship with the Lord.

On the other hand, some women think they are too old to enter a discipling relationship. Again, nothing could be further from the truth. Our homes and churches are suffering from a loss of older men and women pouring their lives and experience into the younger men and women. We are never ready for "retirement" as believers and I hope I go to the grave still just as committed to sharing God's truth as I was when I was a young, inexperienced believer!

Perhaps, no one comes to mind as you consider whom you could join in a discipling relationship. I would encourage you to pray, asking the Lord to bring just the right person into your life. Trust me, He will; I've seen Him do it!

After Steve stepped down from pastoring I must be honest, I was tired! Ten -years of serving alongside him in a church plant had been emotionally and physically exhausting. Although I did some substitute teaching in my new ladies Sunday school class, I mostly just attended church and kept pretty quiet. Then, two years ago, we made the decision to move to North Carolina. As we were packing to move, I began to recognize this funny feeling in my heart. It was the feeling I always felt when I was busy discipling another believer. As the days passed, it became obvious that God was preparing me to get "back in the game." However, here we were moving 16 hours away. I just wasn't sure what God had in mind.

As we made the 16-hour drive in our car, truck, and moving van caravan, I had ample time to pray. I began to ask the Lord to prepare the heart of the woman He wanted me to minister to and I asked Him to open my eyes to recognize her when she appeared. He didn't wait long! Two days after we arrived at our new home, my 14-year old broke the brackets off his braces. (Aren't children helpful that way?) I didn't know of any orthodontists in the area, so I consulted my smart phone and found the nearest orthodontist. When we entered the practice, my son was ushered to the back by a tall, gorgeous redhead. I sat in the waiting room enjoying a few unexpected moments of peace and quiet. 15 minutes later, my son was escorted out with his bracket replaced. The gorgeous red head told me what a sweet boy he was and how happy she was to meet him since she was just a substitute for one day at that office. Then, she said this, "Could we get together for coffee sometime? I just feel like I need to get to know you." (Hmmm... I have a house full of boxes to unload, but ok...) I, of course, agreed and we set a time to meet the next day.

Meg, yes that was the gorgeous redhead's name, and I met at a quaint little coffee shop. I have to tell you, as a 5'2" hobbit-like, mother of eight, the tall, vivacious elf-like woman sitting across from me was a little overwhelming! However, she was the sweetest girl I'd ever met. We quickly learned that we were both Christians and she shared her salvation testimony with me. Meg was a mother of three and she was eager to teach her precious little ones about Jesus. As we talked, I shared scripture and biblical truths and she just drank it in. She asked me how I knew so much and I shared how older women had poured into me when I was her age. I asked her if she'd ever been discipled and that's when the tears started. My tall, beautiful, red haired new friend began to weep as she shared that being discipled had been the prayer of her heart. She was overwhelmed by how God worked all the circumstances to bring us together.

Why do I share this story? I want you to know that discipleship comes directly from the heart of God. He wants His people to encourage, exhort, and excite one another about walking the Christian walk. He wants to teach us truth, not so that we can claim it for ourselves only, but so that we can pass it on to others. He wants to see His people mature and become fruitful. He wants us to become disciple-makers. Yes, first in our homes, but not stopping there! If we want our children to become disciple-makers as well, we must model it for them. They need to see us completely committed to serving others through faithfully sharing our lives with them.

Are you ready to ask the Lord to bring someone into your life? Someone who desires to grow? Someone with whom you can walk the Christian walk? I'm praying that you are! Discipleship is an adventure, and a challenge, and a blessing all rolled into sweet relationship with others!

Now, I don't want to challenge you without equipping you with tools to make your discipleship fruitful. Here are some of the "requirements" I place on any discipleship relationship. Feel free to adjust and adapt this list to your own needs, but remember discipleship isn't just hanging out. No, discipleship needs to be a purposeful implanting of truth from one believer to another. Often, I learn as much from the younger woman I am discipling as they learn from me. Always, I am challenged to "bump it up" in my own walk with the Lord.

Tips for Discipleship:

1. Assign homework! Always, always assign homework. Require that the homework be completed. A negligence to complete homework is a window to the heart. If someone is not committed to completing their homework, they are not committed to being discipled. If they miss once, I remind them that all work must be done. If they miss twice, I tell them that one more miss means we will stop discipling for a time. After three times, I encourage them to contact me again when their time is more conducive to allowing commitment to the discipling relationship.

   I don't ever enforce this rule with harshness! However, it's important to hold a high standard in this area. Without the homework assignment, discipleship can quickly descend into a venting or gossip session and that's just not a good use of anyone's time!

2. Memorize scripture together. Choose verses that fit the need of the woman you are meeting with and commit to memorizing those verses with her. Each week, review all of the verses from the previous week. I often send texts of encouragement throughout the week to strengthen our resolve to get those verses memorized.

3. Find a study you can complete together. Over the years I have used different studies with different women. Some of my favorites are: Experiencing God, by Henry Blackaby, Seeking Him, by Nancy Leigh DeMoss, A Woman After God's Own Heart, By Elizabeth George, and Studies in Character and Bible Basics, which are products of our ministry here at Characterhealth. Work through the study systematically, taking the time necessary to discuss and digest the important teachings.

4. Establish a time for your discipling commitment. Generally speaking, I think 10 weeks is a good length of time to spend together. That doesn't mean that our relationship ends after 10 weeks, it simply means the "formal" part of the discipling will be completed in that timeframe. I have women that I still spend time pouring into and it's been years since we first did our serious studying together.

5. Take time each week to encourage the woman with whom you are meeting. Send cards or notes of encouragement. With today's technology, I suppose I should say texts, emails, or messages...

6. Make time to simply chat outside of your study time. Meg came to my home directly from work each week, so I prepared a simple salad or soup meal for us to share and we spent time just building our relationship. Yes,

I was older than her and we were at different places in our lives, but God knit our hearts together so sweetly.

7. Find out about your friend's family. Know her children's and husbands names. Remember details about her family and encourage her as she seeks to serve them faithfully.

8. Spend time praying with and for the young woman you are discipling. Find out her prayer needs and commit to faithfully praying for them. Help her recognize answers to prayer. Be transparent and share your own needs as well. Nothing binds hearts together more quickly than praying mutually for one another.

9. Finally, exhort, encourage, demand, require, (I can't think of a strong enough word!) the woman you are discipling to commit to discipling someone else. By the third week

of your meetings have her share the name of the person she is going to invite into a discipling relationship. Help her get started in the process. Encourage her to "teach" what she has been learning.

When I was a new believer, it was impressed upon me that I needed to be involved in mentoring/discipling a younger believer. Boy oh boy, was that ever a scary thought! However, I never knew any better. I just grew up in my Christian life believing that every Christian was called to pour into others; it became a part of my spiritual DNA. Thus began my journey of disciple-making. On Mondays, I met with the Young Life staff woman and she poured into me. On Tuesdays, I met with a high school sophomore and taught her everything I'd learned the day before. On Thursdays, she met with a middle school student and relayed everything she'd learned from me. It was a beautiful picture of God's plan for discipleship and it changed all of our lives. To this day, all four of us are still walking faithfully with Jesus and we're intent on sharing our lives with others.

I hope you end this book excited to share your life with a sister in Christ. I'm thrilled as I think of the powerful influence we moms can have on the world around us! I'm encouraged as I consider the practical habits of discipleship our children will learn as they watch us investing in others! God has been so good to all of us. After what He's done for us, is there anything we wouldn't do for Him?

May God be glorified as you pour His truth into the lives of many! And, may God bless you as you disciple your children by developing devotion day by day! Megan Ann Scheibner

RECIPE
SECTION

DINNERS TO MAKE AND FREEZE AHEAD

A stash of dinners tucked away in the freezer can be a lifesaver in more ways than one. On busy days, when you know that time to prepare dinner will be virtually non-existent, the ability to pull an already-prepared dish out of the freezer can save your family from yet another fast-food meal. Frozen meals can make an evening easier for the babysitter and make a dinner date out truly a night off for mom. Perhaps most importantly, meals frozen ahead of time provide us with the opportunity to be ready to minister at a moment's notice.

When a friend or family member has an unexpected need, a frozen meal allows us to meet that need without being forced to run to the store, start from scratch, or find ourselves willing, but sadly unable to serve.

The meals I will share here are not complicated! With 10 people in our family and many extra dinner guests, I save the fancy meals for special occasions. The recipes I will be sharing with you are the favorites in my family and with the young people that so often share our table. We do not have any special dietary restrictions, so I do not use any special or out of the ordinary ingredients. For those of you with special restrictions, feel free to substitute ingredients to meet your family's unique needs.

When freezing meals, I suggest wrapping them first in plastic wrap, then covering the plastic wrap with aluminum foil. Plastic Ziploc bags also make handy storage containers and don't use up much space in the freezer. When you are making and freezing meals to share with someone else, try to use disposable containers so that the recipient of the meal doesn't have to keep track of which dish belongs to which family.

To prepare already frozen meals, take the time to thaw them completely. I keep a monthly menu on the refrigerator to help to keep me on track. Check your menu before going to bed and pull out any meals that must be thawed. Thaw the frozen meals in the refrigerator to avoid any contamination. Before baking the frozen meal, remember to take the plastic wrap off from under the aluminum foil. Sadly, I've learned that lesson from experience!

Most of the freezer meals that I will be sharing here can be completed with a simple tossed salad and some type of bread. If you keep a stash of frozen garlic bread in your freezer, you will always have a bread to deliver with a frozen meal. If the meal is tastier with a different side dish, I will note that side dish beneath the recipe. Most of these dishes serve eight, (I will indicate if this is not the case) so double or halve the recipes as necessary for your family.

> *"Most of the freezer meals that I will be sharing here can be completed with a simple tossed salad and some type of bread."*

Chicken Enchiladas

- 1 Lb. boneless chicken breasts cooked and diced
- 1 can cream of chicken soup
- 1-cup sour cream
- 1 can dice mild green chilies
- 10 flour tortillas, fajita size
- ½ cup salsa
- Cheddar Cheese
- Milk as necessary

In a large bowl, mix together first five ingredients.

Place flour tortillas on a plate and microwave for 15 seconds to soften.

Place approximately 2 TBS of chicken mixture onto flour tortilla. Roll tightly and place, seam side down, in a sprayed 9x13 pan.

Repeat with remaining tortillas placing five per row. They should be squeezed in fairly tightly.

Add enough milk to the remaining chicken mixture to make a slightly runny sauce. Pour the sauce over the

enchiladas and use a spoon to spread evenly.
Sprinkle cheddar cheese over the top of the enchiladas.
Amount of cheese is optional, depending on your
family's tastes.

Cover and freeze. To prepare, thaw completely then bake
covered at 350 degrees for 45 minutes. Uncover for last
15 minutes.

Serve with additional salsa and sour cream. I usually serve
rice and corn with this meal.

Tater-Tot Casserole (or Tater-Tootie as my children say)

- 2 Lbs. ground beef
- 1 can cream of chicken soup
- 1 can evaporated milk
- 1 TBS Worcestershire Sauce
- 3 C frozen green beans
- 1 Large bag frozen potato nuggets

Brown the ground beef and drain well.

Place ground beef in a large bowl. Add all of the remaining ingredients, except for the potato nuggets. Mix well.

Pour mixture into a sprayed 9x13 pan.

Cover the mixture with potato nuggets.

Wrap and freeze. To serve, thaw completely and bake at 375 degrees for 45 minutes. If potato nuggets are not browned at the end of the cooking time, increase the heat to 425 degrees for five minutes.

Chicken Pie

- 1 Lb. boneless chicken breasts, cooked and cubed
- 1 can cream of mushroom soup
- 2 cans Veg-all, drained
- ½ c milk
- ½ tsp. thyme
- Salt and pepper to taste
- Pastry for double crust pie (I use refrigerated crust when I am pressed for time)

Mix first six ingredients in a large bowl.

Place one piecrust in a sprayed deep-dish pie pan.

Pour chicken mixture into piecrust.

Top with second crust. Cut ventilation slits into top crust. Wrap well and freeze.

To serve, thaw completely in refrigerator. Bake uncovered at 350-degrees for one hour. Filling should be bubbling up through the ventilation slits. If edge begins to brown too quickly, cover with aluminum foil for the last 15 minutes of baking.

To bake pie while still frozen, bake at 400 degrees for one hour covered. Reduce heat and continue baking at 350 degrees until filling is bubbling and crust is golden brown.

Assembling these pies is a great service project for pre-teen and teen girls. Put together a dozen pies and fill the church freezer. This will enable the church staff to immediately deliver a helpful meal when needed.

TACO PIE

(This recipe serves 6)

- 1 Lb. ground beef
- ½ c chopped onion
- 2 pkgs. Taco seasoning mix
- ¾ c biscuit baking mix
- 1¼ c milk
- 3 eggs
- 1 c shredded cheddar cheese

Brown ground beef with onion. Drain well.

Mix taco-seasoning mix with ground beef/onion mixture; spoon into a sprayed pie pan.

Combine baking mix, eggs, and milk. Beat with a wire whisk or hand mixer until smooth.

Pour over ground beef mixture in pie pan.

Cover and freeze. Place cheddar cheese into a Ziploc bag and tape to the covered taco pie.

To serve, thaw completely. Bake at 400 degrees for 25 minutes. Sprinkle cheese over the top and bake for 5 minutes longer, or until cheese is melted.

Serve with sour cream, diced tomatoes, and shredded lettuce.

We enjoy this meal with tortilla chips, salad, and corn on the cob.

Super Simple Lasagna

- 4-5 c spaghetti sauce of your choice
- 8 oz. lasagna
- 1 lb. ricotta cheese
- 8 oz shredded mozzarella cheese
- 1 c grated Parmesan cheese

Place 1 cup of the spaghetti sauce in a sprayed 9x13 pan.

Place a layer of UNCOOKED lasagna noodles over the sauce and press them down into the sauce. (For this recipe the noodles do not need to be cooked. Soaking in the sauce while freezing and thawing will sufficiently soften them.)

Top the noodles with some sauce, ricotta, mozzarella, and Parmesan.

Repeat layers pressing each layer down gently.

End with a final layer of lasagna noodles and pour remaining sauce over the top. Make sure all lasagna noodles are covered with sauce.

Sprinkle on remaining mozzarella and parmesan.

Cover and freeze. To serve, thaw completely and bake at 350-degrees for 45-55 minutes. Allow the lasagna to sit for 15 minutes before cutting.

To cook lasagna while still frozen, increase cooking time by one hour. Uncover for last 45 minutes of cooking.

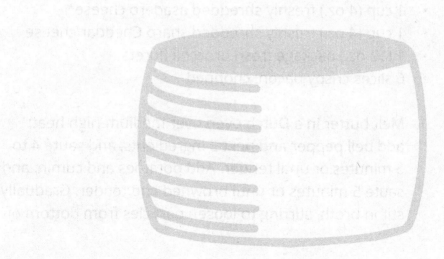

Queso Broccoli Chowder

- 1/4 cup butter
- 1 cup finely chopped red bell pepper
- 1 cup finely chopped onion
- 3 poblano peppers, seeded and finely chopped
- 2 garlic cloves, minced
- 1/2 (20-oz.) package refrigerated Southwestern-style hash brown potatoes
- 1/4 teaspoon ground cumin
- 6 cups chicken broth
- 1/3 cup all-purpose flour
- 1 1/2 cups milk
- 1 cup half-and-half
- 1 cup (4 oz.) freshly shredded asadero cheese*
- 1 cup (4 oz.) freshly shredded sharp Cheddar cheese
- 1 (12-oz.) package fresh broccoli florets
- 6 slices crispy bacon, chopped

1. Melt butter in a Dutch oven over medium-high heat; add bell pepper and next 3 ingredients, and sauté 4 to 5 minutes or until tender. Add potatoes and cumin, and sauté 5 minutes or until browned and tender. Gradually stir in broth, stirring to loosen particles from bottom of

Dutch oven. Bring to a boil; cover, reduce heat to low, and simmer 25 minutes.

2. Whisk together flour and next 2 ingredients. Stir into potato mixture, and cook over medium heat, stirring constantly, 5 minutes or until thickened. Reduce heat to low.

3. Add cheeses, and cook, stirring constantly, until cheeses melt and mixture is thoroughly heated.

4. Place broccoli in a 1-qt. microwave-safe glass bowl. Cover tightly with plastic wrap; fold back a small edge to allow steam to escape. Microwave at HIGH 3 to 4 1/2 minutes or until broccoli is crisp-tender, stirring after 2 minutes. Drain and pat dry. Stir hot broccoli into chowder. Top each serving with sauteed chopped bacon.

5. Cool completely before you freeze.

*Monterey Jack cheese may be substituted.

Chicken Chili:

- 1 pound ground chicken
- 1 yellow onion diced small
- 1 can kidney beans
- 1 cup frozen corn
- 2 16oz cans tomato sauce
- 1 small jalapeno minced
- 1 tsp ground cumin
- 1 tbsp chili powder
- 1 tsp garlic powder

In a medium sauce pan brown the ground chicken. You may need to add a little oil to the pan to keep it from sticking. When the chicken is cooked through add in the onion and sauté until soft and translucent. Add in the jalapeno, cumin, chili powder and garlic powder. Mix until completely incorporated, then add in the kidney beans, corn and tomato sauce. Simmer for about 20 minutes.

Cool completely and freeze in a gallon size freezer bag. To thaw, pull the bag out of the freezer and set in a bowl of warm water for about 6 hours. Heat up on the stove and serve with rice.

Some helpful items to keep in your freezer

There are many foods that can be pre-cooked and frozen, ready to throw into a meal to complete a recipe. A few hours of kitchen time when you are not in a hurry can bring relief during those super busy days or weeks. Following is a list of helpful freezer foods to have on hand. Freeze these items in amounts that you know that you usually use.

Taco meat

- Boneless chicken breast, cooked and cubed
- Ground beef, browned and drained
- Chicken broth
- Spaghetti sauce
- Stuffed shells
- Bread dough
- Cookie dough, just slice and bake
- Cake layers, just frost and serve

Think through the meals your family enjoys most often. What parts of these meals could be frozen ahead to free your time later? We never know when a need will suddenly arise, the wise woman prepares ahead and freezer meals will simplify that preparation!

Slow-Cooker Meals

In Proverbs 31, we are told of the excellent wife and how she used her time and resources. In verse 15 we read about her servant girls and how she cared for them. I don't know about you, but I don't seem to have any servant girls lurking about my house. How about you? Don't despair! We may not have actual girls to help us with our homemaking responsibilities, but thankfully we have many electrical servants to make our job easier. I'm speaking of our "servant" tools: mixers, food processors, bread machines, and most notably, our slow cookers.

There is nothing more encouraging than to come through the door at the end of a busy day and to smell dinner already cooking. Being out of my home is tiring and sometimes I have no energy left to cook. Planning ahead for those days and using my servant, the slow cooker, solves the dilemma of what to feed my hungry family.

Besides being a lifesaver on those busy runaround days, a full slow cooker will enable us to be prepared to practice hospitality on a moment's notice. Have you ever met a new family on a Sunday morning at church and wished you could invite them home to lunch? Too often, we are unable to extend those types of invitations simply because we haven't prepared ahead. Starting your slow cooker early Sunday morning will open up all types of opportunities to invite new families, singles, young adults, lonely elderly folks, and many more to share your food and fellowship.

Consider the purchase of a slow cooker as an investment. As one of the more inexpensive kitchen tools available, perhaps you will want to purchase more than one slow cooker. There are some days that every part of our meal, including dessert, is cooking in a different slow cooker. Many excellent slow cooker recipe books are available and almost any casserole recipe can be converted to a slow cooker recipe.

The recipes that I will be sharing with you are the slow cooker recipes that I use most often. Some are a bit fancier and these I save for Sunday meals. None are difficult and many have the added bonus of leftovers that I can convert into a casserole or soup.

Just a few slow cooking reminders: cut your vegetables to a uniform size in order to ensure even cooking, don't add too much liquid-slow cookers produce more liquid than other types of cooking, add dairy products last, and never store food in your slow cooker. Also, food should not be re-heated in a slow cooker in order to avoid food contamination.

As with freezer meals, having a monthly or weekly menu will help to keep you on track and well prepared for your slow cooker meals. If your slow cooker recipe calls for browned meat or chopped vegetables, make these preparations the night before and just throw everything into the slow cooker in the morning. Even on peaceful stay at home days, using your slow cooker will enable you to spend more time on other projects or perhaps free you up to plan a special treat or dessert.

No, most of us don't have servant girls living in our homes and preparing our meals. However, with the help of our slow cookers, an electric "servant" can do much of the work for us. Make the most of this tool and enjoy the freedom it will bring you.

One Pot Dinner

- 1 Lb ground beef
- ½ Lb. bacon, diced
- 15 oz. can lima beans, drained
- 15 oz. can butter beans, drained
- 2-16 oz. can kidney beans, drained
- 32 oz. can pork and beans, undrained
- 1 medium onion, diced
- 1 tsp. prepared mustard
- 2 tsp. vinegar
- ¾ c. brown sugar
- 1 tsp. salt
- 1 c. ketchup

Brown ground beef and onion until cooked, drain.

Pour beef/onion mixture into slow cooker. Add all other ingredients.

Cover, cook on low for 3-5 hours.

This recipe also freezes well.

Honey Mustard Chicken-This one is so easy!

- 6 Boneless chicken breast halves
- ½ stick butter, melted
- 1 1/3 c honey
- ½ c Dijon mustard

Place chicken in sprayed slow cooker.

In a bowl, combine remaining ingredients. Pour over chicken and make sure that chicken is completely covered.

Cover and cook on LOW for 6 to 8 hours.

I generally serve this dish with rice or egg noodles with the sauce poured over top. Broccoli is a good accompanying vegetable.

Easy Chicken and Stuffing

- 6 Boneless chicken breast halves
- 2-cans cream of chicken soup
- 1-6 oz. box chicken stuffing mix

Place chicken breasts in a sprayed slow cooker and spoon soups over the chicken.

Make stuffing according to package directions. Spoon over chicken and soup.

Cover and cook on LOW for 5-6 hours.

This is so easy and yummy served with Thanksgiving dinner fixings.

Southwest Chicken and Salsa

- 6 Boneless chicken breast halves
- 1-8 oz. package cream cheese, softened
- 1-16 oz. jar salsa (you choose mild, medium, or hot)
- 1 bunch fresh green onions with tops, chopped
- 2 tsp. cumin

Pound chicken breast to flatten.

In a bowl, beat cream cheese until smooth, add salsa, cumin, and onions and mix gently.

Place a heaping spoonful of cream cheese mixture on chicken breast and roll. (You should have leftover cream cheese mixture)

Place chicken rolls in slow cooker, seam side down. Spoon remaining cream cheese mixture over the top.

Cover and cook on LOW for 5-6 hours.

I serve this with rice and fresh steamed green beans. Cornbread is a nice side bread.

Chili

- 2 Lbs. ground beef
- 1 onion, diced
- 2 cans kidney beans, drained
- 2 cans Rotel (mild or medium)
- 1 can diced tomatoes
- 2 can tomato sauce
- 2 TBS chili powder

Brown ground beef and onion, drain.

Place beef/onion mixture into slow cooker. Add remaining ingredients and stir well.

Cover and cook on LOW for 5-6 hours.

Serve this with rice and cornbread. Have sour cream and cheddar cheese available to put on top.

To use leftovers: spoon heated leftover chili into a sprayed pie pan. Prepare one box of Jiffy cornbread mix and spread over the top. Bake at 425 degrees until chili is bubbly and cornbread is golden brown.

Italian Steak Dinner

- 2 Lb. round steak, cut into serving size pieces
- 2 c. fresh mushroom halves
- 2-15 oz. cans stewed tomatoes
- 2-14 oz. cans beef broth
- 2 tsp. Italian seasoning
- 3 TBS quick cooking tapioca

Place beef pieces into sprayed slow cooker.

Combine remaining ingredients and pour over steak.

Cover and cook on LOW for 8-10 hours. To speed up cooking time, start cooking on HIGH for one hour, then reduce heat to LOW for 5-6 hours.

I serve this with linguine or egg noodles and French style green beans.

EASIEST PULLED PORK

- 4-5 Lb. pork butt or shoulder (cheaper cuts work best for this)
- 2 bottles BBQ sauce of your choice
- 1- envelope onion soup mix
- 1 c. water

Place pork roast into sprayed slow cooker. Sprinkle onion soup over the top of the roast. Pour water around roast.

Cover and cook on LOW for 8-10 hours.

Take roast out of the slow cooker and shred meat using two forks. Pour excess liquid out of slow cooker and return meat to cooker.

Pour desired amount of BBQ sauce over meat and mix well.

Serve on rolls. This is the perfect picnic or graduation meal with potato salad, coleslaw, baked beans, and chips!

Sweet and Spicy Ribs

Rather than dealing with BBQ covered children in a restaurant, make these yummy ribs at home!

- 4 Lbs. pork ribs
- 1 bottle chili sauce
- 1 c. ketchup
- ½ c packed brown sugar
- 1/3 c balsamic vinegar
- 2 TBS Worcestershire sauce
- 2 tsp. onion powder
- 1 tsp. salt
- 1 tsp garlic powder
- 1 tsp chili powder
- 1 tsp pepper
- ½ tsp hot pepper sauce (optional)
- ¼ tsp liquid smoke (optional)

Place ribs in a sprayed slow cooker.

Combine remaining ingredients. Pour over ribs.

Cover and cook on LOW for 6-7 hours or until ribs are tender.

Serve with mashed potatoes, corn on the cob, cornbread and lots and lots of NAPKINS!

Easy Chicken Stroganoff:

- 6 chicken thighs, skin off
- 2 cups sour cream
- 1 package French onion soup mix
- 1-cup chicken stock

In a bowl mix together the sour cream, soup mix and chicken stock. Place the chicken thighs in the slow cooker and pour the sour cream mixture over top. Cook on medium fro about 4 hours. The chicken should be falling off the bone.

Serve with egg noodles or rice. Make sure to pour some of the sauce over the noodles!

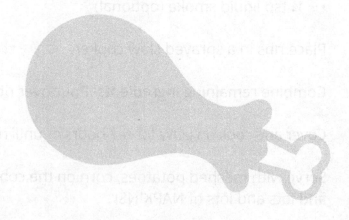

Beef Stew:

- 1 pound beef tips
- 1 large onion diced small
- 3 carrots peeled and cut in ½ inch pieces
- 4 ribs of celery cut in ½ inch pieces
- 4 red potatoes, washed and cut in bite size pieces
- 2 tsp thyme
- 2 tsp garlic powder
- 1 tsp paprika
- 5 cups beef stock
- Salt and pepper to taste

In a skillet brown the beef tips with a little salt and pepper, just to get some color on the out side. Put in the slow cooker with all the other ingredients. Stir well and cook on medium/high for 4 hours.

Serve with crusty bread.

Honey Garlic Chicken:

- 4 boneless skinless chicken thighs
- ½ cup ketchup
- ½ cup soy sauce
- 1/3 cup honey
- ¼ cup Worchestershire sauce
- 3 cloves garlic minced
- 1 large onion diced
- 4 carrots peeled and cut in 1 inch pieces

Dice the onion in a large dice and layer the bottom of the slow cooker with it. Next, peel and cut the carrot and layer it on top of the onion. Season the chicken thighs with salt and pepper and lay on top of the carrots. In a separate bowl, mix together the ketchup, soy sauce, honey, worchestershire sauce, and garlic. Pour over the chicken, evenly. Cook at medium to high heat for 3 ½ hours. This is best served over white rice with a little soy sauce on the side for dipping. If you want to add a little heat to the dish you can mince up one Thai chili and add it to the sauce before cooking.

CASSEROLES AND ONE-POT MEALS

Casseroles and one-pot meals are a huge help in any household, but especially homes with more than two people eating. (I.e. homes with any children!) Both forms of cooking can stretch a small amount of the most expensive ingredients, while combining them with less expensive filler foods. I don't know about you, but our food budget is always higher than I would like for it to be. Casseroles and one-pot meals help to keep us from overspending.

Another benefit of these types of meals is in the way that foods are combined. Our children will often enjoy ingredients in a casserole that they would spurn if the same foods were sitting alone on their plates. Use this dynamic to your advantage. The next time your children complain of some type of food, remind them how much they enjoyed it in the last casserole or one-pot meal.

I have seen several cookbooks on the market that encourage moms to deceive their children by "hiding" disliked foods in the casseroles. This is NOT what I am talking about! Deception is wrong even when it comes to feeding our children! Let your children see what goes into their food, require them to try everything, and encourage them to build an adventurous palate. I have never purposefully left an ingredient out of a recipe because I was afraid my children wouldn't eat it. To do this would be to train them to be picky eaters-manipulative at home and just plain rude in someone else's home.

Most casseroles and one-pot meals are almost complete by themselves. A simple salad and bread will round out many of these recipes. As an added benefit, virtually all casseroles can be assembled ahead of time, and many of them are more flavorful if they are assembled and left in the refrigerator for a few hours before baking. Using morning free time to prepare a dinner casserole will greatly free your afternoon for other activities. To make after-meal clean up easier, remember to always spray your casserole dishes.

A simple casserole with a tossed salad and some muffins makes a great meal to deliver to an ill friend or a new mommy. If the casserole isn't needed right away, the recipient can always place it in the freezer for later use. When I take a casserole to someone else, I always put it in an inexpensive disposable container so that the person receiving the food doesn't have the stress of piled up dishes waiting to be returned all over their kitchen!

Occasionally, when my husband and I have the opportunity to get away by ourselves for an extended period of time, casseroles in the refrigerator make it easier for my children and their caregiver to survive the dinner hour. I just spend a few hours the day before we leave making up casseroles and storing them, then I leave a list of the casseroles and cooking instructions for each dish. When I am away, I can be confident that the children are still eating well and I am not shirking my responsibility toward them!

Invest in a few good casserole dishes. Cheaply made cookware will burn, scratch, and be impossible to clean. Trust me, you'll be frustrated! This is another one of those lessons I learned the hard way as I tried to save money but ended up spending more in the long run to replace my cheap purchases! If you are careful with your good casserole dishes and pots, they are tools that will last you for many years.

Chicken and Stuffing Casserole

- 3 boneless chicken breasts, cooked and cubed
- 1 pkg. Pepperidge Farm stuffing (the blue bag)
- 4 TBS butter, melted
- 1 can cream of mushroom soup
- 1 c sour cream
- 1 c chicken broth

Place stuffing mix in large bowl, pour melted butter over it and mix well.

Place ½ of the stuffing mix in the bottom of a sprayed 9x13 pan.

In a bowl, mix soup and sour cream, add diced chicken and spread over stuffing mix in pan.

Spread remaining stuffing mix over the chicken mixture.

Pour chicken broth over the top of the casserole to moisten.

Bake at 350 degrees until center is bubbly and stuffing mix is lightly browned. Add additional chicken broth if necessary.

I usually serve this casserole with mashed potatoes, peas, and cranberry sauce.

Chicken Divan

- 3 boneless chicken breasts, cooked and cubed
- 1 can cream of chicken soup
- 1 c mayonnaise
- ½ c sour cream
- 4 c frozen broccoli, thawed and patted dry
- 3 c fresh breadcrumbs
- ½ c melted butter
- 2 c shredded cheddar cheese

Combine first five ingredients, mixing well.

Spread chicken mixture into a sprayed 9x13 pan.

Cover casserole with shredded cheese.

Combine breadcrumbs and butter and spread
over cheese.

Bake covered at 350 degrees for 45 minutes. Uncover for
last 15 minutes to brown the breadcrumbs.

Serve this casserole over white rice. I often serve a tossed
salad and blueberry muffins as an accompaniment.

Jambalaya

(this may also be cooked in a slow cooker)

1 tsp lemon pepper
1 tsp garlic powder
2 and ½ lbs. boneless chicken breasts cut in ½ squares
32 oz picante sauce, you choose mild or medium
3 c. frozen salad shrimp
6 TBS oil
2 c. chopped onions
24 oz. Kielbasa cut in ½ in slices
2- cans diced tomatoes
2 and ½ c frozen peas

Sprinkle lemon pepper and garlic powder over the chicken cubes.

Heat oil in a large pot and cook chicken for 5 minutes.

Add onions and sausage and cook for 5 minutes longer.

Stir in picante sauce and diced tomatoes, reduce heat and cook for 12 minutes.

Add peas and shrimp and cook for 5-7 minutes.

This makes a good-sized pot of jambalaya. I serve this over rice with cornbread on the side.

If your family doesn't eat seafood, leave out the shrimp and increase the amount of chicken or Kielbasa.

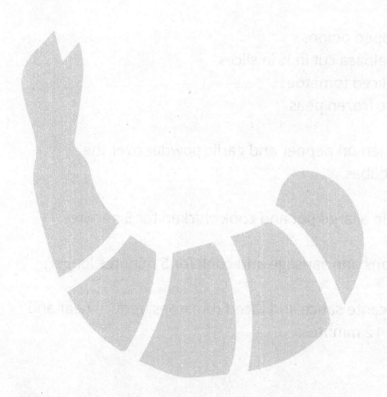

CRESCENT TACO PIE

- 1 can crescent rolls
- 1 small bag of nacho chips, crushed
- 1 lb. ground beef
- 1-8 oz. can tomato sauce
- ½ c. water
- 1 pkg. taco seasoning mix
- 1 c. sour cream
- 1 c. shredded mozzarella

Brown ground beef and drain.

Add tomato sauce, water, and taco seasoning. Cook over medium heat for 5 minutes.

Unroll crescent rolls and line a sprayed pie pan.

Layer other ingredients in this order: ½ crushed chips, ground beef mixture, sour cream, cheese, and remaining chips.

Bake at 375 degrees for 25 minutes.

Serve this with a tossed salad and corn on the cob.

Leftovers reheat beautifully, I always make two pies at once so that there will be leftovers!

Easy Swedish Meatballs

- 16 oz. medium or wide egg noodles
- 4 c. broccoli, fresh or frozen is fine
- 2 can beef broth
- 48 already cooked meatballs
- 6 TBS apple juice
- 2 c. sour cream
- 4 TBS cornstarch
- 6 TBS cold water
- Salt and pepper to taste

In a large pot of boiling water, cook noodles, uncovered, for 4 minutes.

Place broccoli on top of the noodles and continue to cook for 3 more minutes.

In a large skillet, bring broth to a boil. Add meatballs and apple juice and cook, uncovered, until the meatballs are heated completely.

Reduce heat to low.

Slide meatballs to one side of skillet; add sour cream

on the other side. Stir with a whisk until sour cream is smooth, and then add meatballs to sour cream.

Mix the cornstarch and water until there are no lumps. Add to skillet and stir until thickened, about 1 minute.

Drain the noodles and broccoli. Mix with meatball mixture in a large pasta bowl.

Add salt and pepper to taste.

Cheesy Salsa, Beef, and Rice

This recipe serves 6

- 1 c long grain rice, cooked
- 1 lb. ground beef
- 1 TBS oil
- 1 large onion
- 1 c. chopped green, red, or yellow pepper
- 2 cloves minced garlic
- 2 c frozen corn
- 1 can diced tomatoes
- 1 jar salsa cheese sauce

Brown ground beef, onion, pepper, and garlic in the oil. Drain any extra fat.

Add the corn and tomatoes with their juice. Stir to mix. Reduce heat to low and simmer for 5 minutes.

Add the cooked rice and salsa cheese sauce, stir well.

Heat thoroughly.

This is good served with a tossed salad and muffins.

Beef Bake with a Biscuit Crown

- 1 lb. ground beef
- 1 can sliced mushrooms
- 1 can (2.8 oz.) French fried onions, crumbled
- 2 c. frozen mixed vegetables
- 1 can cream of celery soup
- 1 c. sour cream, divided
- 1 can refrigerated biscuits
- 1 egg, beaten
- 1 tsp. celery seed
- ½ tsp. salt

Brown ground beef and drain.
Place ½ of the beef in a sprayed 2-quart casserole dish.
Add mushrooms, 2/3 of the onions and all of the frozen vegetables.

Top with remaining beef.

In a saucepan, combine soup and ½ cup of the sour cream, heat through and pour over beef.

Cut each biscuit in half and arrange, cut side down, around the edge of the casserole dish.

In a bowl, combine egg, celery seed, salt, and remaining sour cream. Drizzle over the biscuits.

Bake, uncovered, at 375 degrees for 25-30 minutes or until biscuits are golden brown.

HUNGARIAN GOULASH

- ¼ c all-purpose flour
- 1 TBS Paprika
- 1 ½ tsp salt
- ½ tsp hot paprika
- ½ tsp pepper
- 2 lbs. beef stew meat
- 4 TBS vegetable oil, divided
- 1 large onion, chopped
- 4 cloves garlic, minced
- 2 cans (14oz) beef broth
- 1 can (15oz) stewed tomatoes
- 1 c water
- 1 TBS marjoram leaves, crushed
- 1 large green pepper, chopped
- 3 c egg noodles
- Sour cream

Combine flour, both paprika's, salt, and black pepper in a re-sealable bag. Add ½ of the beef, seal and shake well. Repeat with remaining beef.

Heat 4-½ tsps oil in Dutch oven over medium heat. Brown ½ of the beef and transfer to a bowl. Repeat with another 4 ½ tsp oil and beef.

Heat remaining 1 TBS of oil in Dutch oven then add onion and garlic. Cook until tender.

Return beef, any juices, and remaining ingredients, except for green pepper, to Dutch oven. Bring to a boil, then reduce heat and cook covered over low heat for 1 ½ hours or until meat is tender.

When meat is tender, stir in green pepper and noodles. Cover and simmer until noodles are tender, about 8 minutes, stirring once.

Serve in bowls with a dollop of sour cream.

Cheeseburger Soup

(My All-Time Most Requested Recipe)

- 1 lb. ground beef
- ¾ cup each: chopped onion, shredded carrots, diced celery
- 1 tsp. each: basil and parsley
- 4 TBS butter, divided
- 3 cups chicken broth
- 4 cups diced potatoes
- ¼ c flour
- 16 oz. Velveeta
- 1 ½ cups milk
- ¾ tsp salt
- ¼ tsp pepper
- ½ c sour cream

In a large saucepan, brown beef and set aside. Wipe pan and sauté onion, carrots, celery, basil, and parsley, in 1 TBS butter. Add broth, potatoes, and beef. Bring to a boil. Reduce heat and simmer 20 minutes or until potatoes are cooked.

In a small skillet, melt 3 TBS butter, add flour to make

a roux. Stir for 3 minutes. Add to soup and return soup to a boil. Cook for 2minutes. Return heat to low. Stir in cheese, milk, salt, and pepper. When cheese is melted, add sour cream.

Super Simple Family Favorites

Here they are...the Scheibner family favorite recipes. All of these recipes are a regular part of our monthly menus. You'll notice that everyone will love some of these recipes; while other recipes are "child adored" and "adult accepted!" None of these recipes are difficult and most of them use ingredients that I always have in my freezer, refrigerator, or pantry.

I would encourage you to keep a record of your own family favorite recipes. As you look back at some of the foods your children loved when they were young, your whole family will enjoy a good laugh. One year, as we were eating the leftovers out of the refrigerator in preparation to ending our family vacation, we tried a "new" dish. I took leftover sloppy joe meat, poured it over spaghetti noodles, and served the whole thing on hamburger buns. Thus the invention of the "sloppy-joe-spaghetti-sandwich." One of my daughters absolutely loved this sandwich and declared that she would be serving it at her wedding reception someday. Needless to say, she's never lived it down and we are looking forward to a little surprise at her rehearsal dinner...

Take the time to make "family favorite" cookbooks for your daughters to take with them when they leave home for their own kitchens. Remember your sons as well. Providing the new brides with some of your son's favorite recipes will give them the opportunity to please and surprise their new husbands. Sharing family favorite recipes can be a fun part of passing on your children's special heritage to their new spouses.

POTATOES AND KIELBASA

To serve 8

- 2 packages polska kielbasa
- 12 russet potatoes
- 2 green peppers
- 2 onions
- 1 stick butter

Scrub potatoes and cut into eighths, place in a large roasting pan.

Chop green peppers and onions into a large bite-sized pieces, scatter over the potatoes.

Cut kielbasa into 3 inch segments and place on top of the potatoes, onions, and green peppers.

Cut the butter into small pieces and scatter over the pan. Pour in 1 cup of water. Cover with foil and bake at 350 degrees for one hour or until potatoes are soft.

Sloppy Joes

I always double this recipe and freeze some for later

2 lbs. ground beef
1 green pepper, diced
1 large onion, diced
1 (15oz) can of tomato sauce
1 bottle of chili sauce
1 TBS mustard
1 TBS cider vinegar
¼ c brown sugar (add more if you like sweeter sloppy joes)

Brown ground beef and drain fat.

Add remaining ingredients and simmer over low heat for 20 minutes. Can also be put into a slow cooker on low heat.

Serve on hamburger buns.

This recipe is great to serve a crowd. I have a whole crew of college boys that beg for containers of sloppy joe to keep in their freezers! This doesn't take much longer than the canned variety and is so much tastier.

Hobo Packets

- 1 packet per person, plan ingredients accordingly
- Ground beef
- Potato
- Carrot
- Onion

For each packet, lay a 12 inch piece of aluminum foil on the counter.

Form a hamburger and place in the center of the foil.

Thinly slice a potato over the hamburger.

Thinly slice a carrot over the potato.

Add 3-4 onion rings, salt, and pepper.

Close the packet tightly, place on a cookie sheet, and bake at 350 degrees for 45 minutes.

My kids just love these! I think it is the novelty of the individual packets that makes them seem so special.

Creamed Chicken

You could also use ham, sausage, tuna, or ground beef for this one, recipe serves 6

- 6 TBS butter
- 6 TBS flour
- 1 tsp salt
- 1/8 tsp pepper
- 1 ½ c chicken broth
- 1 c milk
- 1 c cooked, diced chicken
- optional: ½ c frozen peas, 1 small can mushrooms

Melt butter and whisk in flour, salt, and pepper, to make a roux.

Remove from heat and stir in chicken broth and cream. Bring to a boil and boil for one minute, stirring constantly.

Add chicken and any optional ingredients.

I serve this over hot biscuits with mashed potatoes, cranberry sauce and candied carrots. Could also be served over cornbread.

This recipe is so simple, but I have a whole group of young friends that check our menu to see when this is being served, just so that they can show up to dinner!

Orange Pork Chops:

- 8 pork chops
- 2 c orange juice
- ½ c brown sugar
- 2 tsp salt
- 2 tsp dry mustard
- ½ tsp lemon pepper

Do not pre-brown the pork chops! Place chops in a baking dish. Mix remaining ingredients well and pour over chops.

Bake covered at 350 for 1 ½ hours, adding additional orange juice if necessary.

These are really good served with rice with the sauce poured over top.

Parmesan Chicken:

- ½ c butter, melted
- 2 tsp Dijon mustard
- 1 tsp Worcestershire sauce
- ½ tsp salt
- 1 c dry bread crumbs
- ½ c Parmesan cheese
- 8 boneless chicken breasts

In a pie plate, combine butter, mustard, Worcestershire sauce, and salt.

In another pie plate, combine bread crumbs and Parmesan cheese.

Dip chicken in butter mixture, then crumb mixture, then place in an ungreased baking pan. Drizzle with any remaining butter mixture or melt ¼ c more to drizzle over the top.

Bake a 350 degrees for 45 minutes or until chicken is done.

I serve this with chicken flavored rice or couscous and corn.

Beefy Enchiladas

- 1 lb ground beef
- 1 can chili beans, undrained
- 1 medium onion, chopped
- 1 can enchilada sauce, divided
- 4 oz. salsa, divided
- Vegetable oil
- 8 flour tortillas
- 1 c shredded cheddar cheese
- optional: sliced olives
- Brown beef and onions together, drain. Stir in beans, ½ can enchilada sauce, and 1 TBS salsa.

Warm the flour tortillas in the microwave.

Top each tortilla with 2/3 c beef mixture. Roll up and place seam-side down in a sprayed baking dish. Drizzle with remaining enchilada sauce and salsa. Sprinkle with cheese and olives, if desired.

Bake at 350 degrees for 20-25 minutes.

Serve this with sour cream on top. I like to have Spanish rice and corn on the cob as side dishes.

Chicken Pasta Alfredo:

- 4 boneless skinless chicken breasts
- 2 tbsp olive oil
- 2 cups heavy cream
- 1 onion diced very small
- 3 cloves of garlic minced fine
- 2 cups grated Parmesan cheese
- 1 large handful of basil chopped
- ½ pound fettuccini pasta
- 3 cup broccoli florets

The chicken in this recipe can be prepared many ways. My favorite way is to place it inside a storage bag with the oil, salt and pepper. Using a rolling pin pound the chicken until it is about ½ an inch thick. Then grill it on both sides for about 4 minutes per side. Set aside for later. In a pot sauté the onion and garlic until translucent, pour in the 2 cups of heavy cream. Let the cream simmer until it has reduced by half.

Slowly add in the cheese, one handful at a time. Make sure that you stir thoroughly after each addition of cheese to make sure it is completely melted.

In another pot bring about 8 cups of water to a boil. Put in the broccoli and let it blanche for about 2 minutes. Remove from the water and put in your pasta to cook. Strain the pasta when tender. Dump the pasta and the broccoli in with the sauce. Slice the chicken and serve on top of the pasta.

Best served with a warm piece of crusty bread.

Homemade Pizza Dough

This is yummy!

- In a large bowl or mixer place:
- 2 c. warm water
- 2 Tbs. brown sugar
- 2 Tbs. yeast
- Whisk together and let get bubbly, approximately 10 minutes.

Add:
- 2 Tbs. olive oil
- 1 ½ tsp. salt
- 5 c (approx) flour

Mix well and then knead for 5 minutes. You can do this by hand or in a mixer. Just add flour until the mixer cleans the side of the bowl or until you cannot add more by hand and the dough is not sticky.

Cover and let rise for 15 minutes. This makes two large pizzas.

Bake at 450 degrees until golden and crispy. Although I own pizza stones, we prefer to use the inexpensive pizza screens which allow the pizza to be crisp the whole way across the bottom.

BBQ Bacon Pizza

1. Homemade Pizza Dough
2. 1 bottle of your favorite bbq sauce
3. 8 slices of bacon chopped
4. 1 red onion sliced thin
5. 3 cups mozzarella cheese
6. 1 cup cheddar cheese

Spread the bbq on the pizza crust, then layer the cooked chopped bacon, onion and cheeses. Bake in a 475 degree oven for 12-15 minutes, or until crust is golden brown and cheese is melted. Slice and serve!

Salisbury Steak:

- 2 pounds ground beef
- 1 yellow onion diced small
- 2 cloves of garlic minced
- 2 eggs
- 1 cup of breadcrumbs
- 1 cup grated Parmesan cheese
- 1 bunch of parsley chopped
- 10 button mushrooms sliced thin
- 3 cups beef stock
- 2 tbsp butter
- 2 tbsp flour
- salt and pepper to taste

In a mixing bowl add together the top 7 ingredients. Mix thoroughly. Break off small handfuls and shape into patties. This will resemble hamburger patties. Sear in a skillet for 2 minutes on each side. Remove the meat and add butter to the skillet. Put in the mushrooms and sauté until lightly browned all over. Add in the flour and stir to combine. After the flour has been combined and cooked for about 2 minutes pour in the beef stock. Stir briskly until the gravy starts to thicken.

Place the steaks in a 9x13 pan and pour the gravy over top. Cook in a 400 degree oven for about 15 minutes.
Best served with mashed potatoes.

Fun and
Easy Sides

Twice-Baked Potatoes

This recipe is so easy and very handy to have in the freezer.

- Large Russet baking potatoes (as many as desired)
- Milk
- Butter
- Sour cream
- Salt
- Shredded cheddar cheese
- Optional ingredients: bacon, chives

Poke potatoes several times with a fork. Bake at 400 degrees for one hour, or until soft when squeezed.

Cut open potatoes and scoop out the center leaving a thin rim of potato skin intact.

Place potato centers in a large bowl. Add enough butter, salt, sour cream, and milk, to achieve a smooth consistency. Beat with a hand beater until smooth.

Fold in cheddar cheese to taste.

PERFECT MASHED POTATOES:

- 6 medium to large russet potatoes
- 1 stick of butter
- 1/3-cup of milk
- 1 tbsp salt
- 2 tsp black pepper
- 1 tsp garlic powder

Peel and dice the potatoes into bite size pieces. Put the potatoes in a large pot and cover with water, bring to a rolling boil and cook until they fall apart when a fork is inserted in a piece. Strain completely and put back in the pot. Using either a potato masher or a hand mixer (I prefer the hand mixer), begin to whip the potatoes. Add in the butter and the milk and whip until soft peaks appear. Add in the salt, pepper and garlic powder to taste. Potatoes love salt! It will take more than you are used to, but trust me on this, use the salt! If you use a potato masher to make these, then at the very end take a whisk and stir for a minute or two. It will add a little air to the potatoes and make them light and fluffy.

Sweet Corn Grits:

- 2 cups sweet corn, frozen is fine
- 2 sticks of butter
- 1 medium yellow onion, diced very small
- 2 cloves of garlic minced
- 4 cups of milk or cream
- 2 cups of water
- 2 cups white grits (not instant cook, 5 minute is best)

In a large pot melt the butter; throw in the diced onion and garlic and sauté until translucent, try not to get any color on the onions.

Add in the corn and sauté for 2 minutes. Stir in the grits and toast for 1 minute. Pour in half the cream and let the grits soak it all up. Stir constantly for about 4 minutes. Repeat the process with the rest of the cream and then the water. After the water has cooked into the grits and they are smooth and creamy looking, add salt and pepper to taste. Enjoy!

Roasted Green Beans:

- 1 pound fresh green beans, ends removed
- 2 cloves garlic minced
- 2 tbsp olive oil
- 1 tsp salt
- 1 tsp pepper
- ½ crushed red pepper flakes

Mix everything together, making sure the green beans are really coated well with the oil. Bake in a 400 degree oven for 10 minutes or until the beans are cooked through but still have a tiny bit of crunch.

Dill Carrots:

- 4 carrots peeled and cut into 1 inch pieces
- 4 tbsp butter
- 2 tbsp dill (I use dried dill, but fresh works just as well.)
- 1/3-cup chicken stock
- Salt and pepper to taste

Bring a pot of water to a rolling boil, put the carrots in the water and blanch until fork tender. In a sauté pan, melt the butter and throw in the dill. Add the carrots and coat with the butter. Pour in the chicken stock and let it cook down for about 3-4 minutes to create a nice glaze on the carrots. Season with salt and pepper and enjoy!

Brownie Cheesecake Cookies:

- 12 ounces (2 cups) semi-sweet chocolate, chopped
- 4 oz, 8 tablespoon or 1 stick, unsalted butter
- 3 eggs
- 1 1/2 teaspoons vanilla extract
- 1 cup sugar (7 oz)
- 1/2 cup all-purpose flour (2.5 oz)
- 1 1/2 teaspoons baking powder
- 1/4 teaspoon salt
- 6 ounces (1 cup) semisweet chocolate chips
- 1 8oz package of cream cheese
- ¼ cup sugar

Sift the dry ingredients of flour, baking powder and salt together, set aside.

In the top of a double boiler set over hot water, melt the semi-sweet chocolate and butter together. Once they are completely melted, take off the pot and let sit for few minutes.

Using an electric mixer, beat the eggs and vanilla in a mixing bowl until frothy. Slowly add the sugar and beat until the mixture until smooth. Add the melted chocolate mixture. Stir to combine. Add flour mixture, just enough to combine. You may see a few specks of flour, which is fine. Fold in remaining chocolate chips and walnuts.

In a seperate bowl mix together the cream cheese and sugar. Stir into the dough, but leave some lumps.

The dough will be very thin like cake batter. Cover and chill in the refrigerator for about an hour until dough firms up. Set the oven to 350 degrees. Line several baking sheets with baking parchment. Bake for 10-12 minutes until the tops begin to crack.

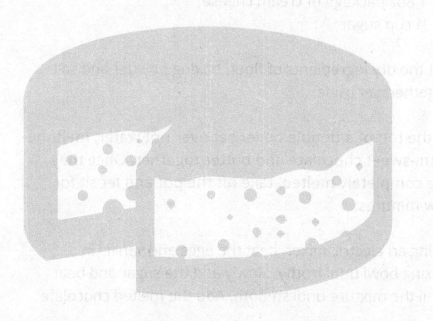

CREAMED CORN:

- 6 cobs of corn
- 2 cups heavy cream
- 1-cup milk
- 1 large onion diced small
- 2 ribs of celery diced small
- 1 stick of butter
- 1 tsp thyme
- 1 tsp paprika
- 1 tsp garlic powder
- Salt and pepper to taste

Peel the corn and remove the stem. Shave the kernels off the cob. I place the corn upright into a large bowl and shave into the bowl, this keeps the kernels from going all over the place. In a large pot sauté the onion and celery with the butter. When the onions are soft add in the shaved corn and sauté for another 2 minutes. Add in the thyme, paprika, garlic power and cream. Cook the cream down by about half and then add in the milk and repeat. Taste and add salt and pepper.

CANDIED CARROTS:

- 4 carrots peeled and cut into 1 inch pieces
- 1 stick of butter
- ½-cup brown sugar
- 2 tsp thyme

Blanche the carrots in a pot of boiling water until fork tender. In a sauté pan melt the butter and stir in the brown sugar and thyme. Mix in the carrots and toss until thoroughly coated.

CINNAMON APPLES:

- 7 granny smith apples
- ½ -cup butter melted
- 1-cup sugar
- ½ cup cinnamon red-hot candies
- ¼ cup water

Peel and core the apples and slice into nice thick slices. In a sauté pan melt the butter over medium heat and then add in the apples. Sprinkle the sugar over the top and stir. Add in the cinnamon candies and stir until incorporated. Pour in the water and cover the pan to steam cook the apples. When the apples and able to be cut with a fork they are done. Stir again gently to insure the cinnamon flavor covers all the apples.

Loaded Mashed Potatoes:

Use the Mashed Potatoes recipe above

- 2 cups shredded white cheddar cheese
- 1 cup sour cream
- 4 green onions sliced thin
- 8 slices of bacon crisped and chopped
- 2 tbsp butter melted

In a big bowl mix everything but the butter together. Put in a greased 9x13 pan. Drizzle the melted butter on top and bake in a 375-degree oven for 10-15 minutes. The top should start to be light golden brown.

Shaved Brussels Sprouts:

- 1 pound of brussels sprouts
- 10 slices of bacon
- 1 yellow onion sliced thin
- 4 tbsp butter
- ¼ balsamic vinegar
- ½ cup chicken stock
- ½ cup dried cranberries

Cut the end off of the sprout and using either a food processor, mandolin, or knife shave them very thin. Chop the uncooked bacon into small pieces and crisp in sauté pan. After the bacon is crisp remove it from the pan and begin to sauté the onions. Turn the heat down and slowly caramelize the onions. Once the onions are a nice brown turn the heat back up and add in the shaved sprouts and bacon. Sauté everything together until the sprouts are just starting to crisp.

In a separate pot, bring the vinegar and stock to a boil. Once it is boiling add in the dried cranberries and allow to boil for 5 minutes. Pour over the sprouts and let the liquid reduce. Serve warm and enjoy!

Desserts

Dinner is never complete without something sweet to finish off the night. Here are some recipes that are either family favorites or recipes that I have developed over the years in the restaurant world. Desserts are meant to be whimsical, so have fun with the recipes. Feel free to change them up and make them your own!

Desserts can often be made ahead of time and are a great way for kids to get involved in the kitchen. Some of my favorite memories growing up are of making cookies or pies with my mom and sisters. Every year at Thanksgiving we all get together and the women gather in the kitchen. We blast Taylor Swift, dance, and cook together. Everyone chips in to peel apples, mix cookies, or whip cream.

Take the time to make dessert. It is fun and a great way to prolong the dinner hour. These days that we have at home with our families are short. Take advantage of every opportunity to grow closer together and closer to God.

Chocolate Hazelnut Tarts:

- 4 oz semisweet chocolate (I use bakers)
- ¼ cup heavy cream
- 2 cups heavy cream (whipped)
- 2 cups Nutella
- Phyllo Dough
- 1 cup chopped hazelnuts
- 1 stick of melted butter

Using a double boiler melt the chocolate, add in the ¼-cup cream at the end and stir to combine. Put in the refrigerator to cool for about 15 minutes. You want it to be cool be not starting to firm up. In a separate bowl whip the heavy cream until hard peaks form. Slowly fold the chocolate in to the whipped cream, very gently so that the cream doesn't lose its volume. Place in the refrigerator to set for 20 minutes.

Meanwhile, melt the butter and brush over the Phyllo one sheet at a time. You want to have three or four layers oh Phyllo when you are done. Cut the dough into 12 pieces and press down into a greased muffin tin. Bake in a 350 degree oven for 10-12 minutes or until golden brown. Remove the tart shell from the muffin tin and let cool.

Take a spoonful of the nutella and layer it in the bottom of the shell. Next take a scoop of the chocolate mousse and put it in the shell. Finish the tart with a sprinkle of the chopped hazelnuts.

Store in the refrigerator until you are ready to serve.

Gorilla Bread:

- 1/2 cup sugar
- 3 tsp cinnamon
- ½ cup butter
- 1 cup brown sugar, packed
- 8 oz. cream cheese
- 2-12 oz. cans refrigerated biscuits
- 1 ½ cup chopped nuts

Spray a bundt pan.

Mix white sugar and cinnamon

Melt butter and brown sugar over low heat, set aside

Cut cream cheese into 20 cubes

Flatten biscuits and sprinkle with ½ tsp of cinnamon/sugar

Wrap each biscuit around cream cheese cube

Sprinkle ½ cup nuts into pan

Place ½ of biscuits into pan

Sprinkle with cinnamon/sugar

Pour ½ of melted butter over biscuits

Sprinkle ½ cup nuts

Layer remaining biscuits, cinnamon/sugar, and butter

Sprinkle with remaining nuts.

Bake at 350 for 30 minutes. Cool 5 minutes. Place plate on top and invert.

Apple Crisp:

- 10 granny smith apples
- 2 cups oatmeal
- 1- cup flour
- 1-cup butter
- ½ cup sugar
- 2 tsp cinnamon
- 1 tsp nutmeg
- 1 tsp ginger

Peel and core the apples and slice to a medium thickness. Grease a 9x13 pan and lay the apples in it. In a bowl mix together the flour, oatmeal, sugar and spices. Cut in the butter using a dough cutter or a fork. When to mixture resembles tiny pebbles sprinkle it over the top of the apples. Bake for 30-40 minutes until the apples begin to bubble and the topping is golden brown. Serve warm with vanilla ice cream.

Peach biscuit Cobbler:

- 8 cups of frozen peaches
- 2 cups of sugar
- 2 cups of cherries
- 2 tsp cinnamon
- 1 tsp nutmeg
- ½ tsp cloves
- 1 batch of your favorite biscuits (I honestly use the pop can type for this)

In a medium pot heat together the peaches, sugar, cherries, and spices. Once the sugar is completely melted and everything is warm pour it into a greased 9x13 pan. Place the biscuits on top and bake in a 350-degree oven until the biscuits are golden brown, about 15-20 minutes. Serve warm.

Recipes That Teach Spiritual Truths

In this final section, I will be sharing recipes that you can utilize to celebrate special holidays or simply teach a spiritual lesson. Backing up our teaching with hands on activities, such as making a special treat, will help our children to deeply incorporate and remember the lessons that we are teaching them.

Although some of these recipes are a little complicated, if you follow the directions carefully, you should have good results. Some of the recipes we use year after year, while others were a once and done lesson. Use your imagination to develop more and more recipes to teach spiritual lessons. Ask your children for their ideas as well. For some of these recipes, you may want to act out the bible story involved and have the final product of your recipe as the treat at the conclusion of the story.

Along with incorporating these recipes, I would strongly urge you to purchase or create a "You Did Great" plate. With this plate, you can teach your children the priceless quality of encouragement. Use the plate to affirm your children's good character and special achievements. Be generous with the plate, but don't use it to praise your children for simply doing what is required of them. It's easy to find reasons to award the You Did Great plate, but may I encourage you to look beyond the obvious successes, i.e. sports achievements, good grades, or musical accomplishments? Instead, concentrate on using the plate to reward good character. When you see a child being generous, or compassionate, or kind, take the opportunity to encourage more of that behavior by rewarding them with the You Did Great plate.

When I award a child with the plate, I take the opportunity to make it a family occasion. I fill the plate with the recipient's dinner and bring it to the table without saying who will be receiving the plate. Seeing me fill the plate starts the buzz of conversation as the children begin discussing who "did great." When I get to the table, I stand beside the deserving child and ask them if they know why they are receiving the plate. Oftentimes, they don't even realize what they've done that is worthy of recognition. I share with the family the positive character quality or qualities that I saw being exhibited and then, I present the plate. The whole family applauds and even when they blush, the rewarded child feels encouraged and affirmed. Use the plate with the adults in the family as well. Give your children the responsibility of looking for opportunities to present mom or dad with the "You Did Great" plate.

Since I first wrote this book, I've found an even more powerful and effective way to utilize the You Did Great plate. Instead of always being the person to recognize achievement and award the plate, I opened up the opportunity for the other children to present the You Did Great plate, as well. I encouraged them to observe their brothers and sisters and to then come tell me when they saw great character being exhibited. This accomplished two very powerful outcomes. First, my children became very attuned to recognizing the practice of good character. In order to reward someone else, they had to first understand what good character looked like in action. The second positive outcome was even more powerful. As my children began to look for opportunities to "catch one another doing great," the level of tattling and tale bearing in our home saw a dramatic reduction. As they became intent on rewarding one another's good behavior, the temptation to focus on noticing bad behavior just disappeared. When I gave them the opportunity to reward one another I hadn't envisioned those outcomes, but what a blessing it has been to see the positive change in our family dynamic.

A You Did Great plate doesn't have to be expensive or fancy. Just find a special way to reward positive character and then remember to be consistent in using it. The only way to fail with a You Did Great plate is by failing to implement it on a consistent basis. This one little investment can yield great spiritual fruit in your children's lives and character.

Have fun with these recipes and use them as a springboard to even bigger projects and learning opportunities.

> *"A You Did Great plate doesn't have to be expensive or fancy. Just find a special way to reward positive character and then remember to be consistent in using it."*

EASTER STORY COOKIES

- 1 c whole pecans
- 1 tsp vinegar
- 3 egg whites
- Pinch of salt
- 1 c sugar
- Ziploc baggie
- Wooden spoon
- Tape
- Bible

Pre-heat the oven to 300 degrees!!!!!

1. Place the pecans in the Ziploc baggie. Have your children beat them with the wooden spoon until they are in pieces. Use this time to explain that after Jesus was arrested, He was beaten by the Roman soldiers. Read John 19:1-3.

2. Put the vinegar into a mixing bowl. Let each child smell the vinegar. Explain that when Jesus was on the cross and became thirsty, He was offered vinegar to drink. Read John 19:28-30.

3. Add the egg whites to the vinegar. The eggs represent life. Explain that Jesus gave His life so that we could have life. Read John 10:10-11.

4. Sprinkle a little salt into each of your children's hands and let them taste it. Put the rest into the bow. Explain that this represents the salty tears shed by Jesus' followers and the bitterness of our own sin. Read Luke 23:27.

5. Point out that so far the ingredients are not very appetizing. Add 1 cup of sugar. Explain that the sweetest part of the story is that Jesus died because He loves us. He wants us to know and belong to Him. Read Psalm 34:8 and John 3:16.

6. Beat the egg whites with a mixer on high speed for 12-15 minutes, until stiff peaks form. Explain that the color white represents the purity in God's eyes of those whose sins have been washed clean by Jesus. Read Isaiah 1:18 and John 3:1-3.

7. Fold in the broken nuts. Drop by teaspoons onto a wax paper lined cookie sheet. Explain that each mound represents the rocky tomb where Jesus' body was laid to rest. Read Matthew 27:57-60.

8. Put the cookie sheet in the oven, close the door and turn the oven off.

9. Give each child a piece of tape and seal the door. Explain that Jesus' tomb was sealed. Read Matthew 27:65-66.

10. Go to bed. Explain that they may feel sad to leave the cookies in the oven overnight and that Jesus' followers were sad when the tomb was sealed. Read John 16:20-22.

11. On Easter morning, open the oven and give everyone a cookie. Point out the cracked surface and then take a bite; the cookies are hollow! On the first Easter, Jesus' followers were amazed to find His tomb empty. Finish by reading Matthew 28:1-9.

Resurrection Rolls

- 1 can crescent rolls
- 8 large marshmallows
- ¼ c melted butter
- 2 TBS ground cinnamon
- 2 TBS sugar

Preheat oven to 400 degrees. Lightly grease a baking sheet.

Separate crescent rolls into triangles.

In a small bowl, mix cinnamon and sugar.

Dip a marshmallow into the melted butter, then roll in the sugar mixture. Place on center of dough triangle.

Carefully wrap the dough around the marshmallow and pinch seams to seal tightly.
Repeat with remaining marshmallows and dough.

Bake until golden brown, about 14 minutes.

The rolls become hollow as they bake, representing the empty tomb on Easter morning.

HAMENTASCHEN OR HAMAN'S HATS

When you are studying the book of Esther with your children, take the time to make these traditional Purim treats! More information on Purim can be easily found via the internet.

- 2/3 c butter
- ½ c sugar
- 1 egg
- ¼ c smooth orange juice
- 1 c white flour
- 1 c wheat flour
- 2 tsp baking powder
- 1 tsp cinnamon
- Various preserves, fruit butters and/or pie fillings

Blend butter and sugar thoroughly. Add the egg and blend well.

Add flour ½ c at a time, blending well after each addition. Add the baking powder and cinnamon with the last half cup of flour.

Refrigerate the batter overnight.

The next day, roll the batter out between two sheets of wax paper lightly dusted with flour. Roll as thin as possible.

Cut out 3 or 4 inch circles.

Put a dollop of the filling of your choice in the middle of each circle.

Fold up the sides to make a triangle, folding the last corner under the starting corner.

Bake at 350 degrees for 15-20 minutes. Traditional fillings are poppy seed and prune, but all fillings work well.

HOT CROSS BUNS

Although these buns were probably originally used in pagan ceremonies, the early Christian church made them "Christianized." Queen Elizabeth I passed a law limiting the bun's consumption to proper religious ceremonies, such as Christmas and Easter.

- 1 c milk
- 2 TBS yeast
- ½ c sugar
- 2 tsp salt
- 1/3 c butter, melted and cooled
- 1 tsp cinnamon
- ½ tsp nutmeg
- 4 eggs
- 5 c flour
- 1 1/3 c currants or raisins
- 1 egg white

Heat milk to 110 degrees. Pour warm milk into mixing bowl and sprinkle yeast over top. Mix to dissolve and then let sit for 5 minutes.

With mixer running at low speed, add sugar, salt, butter, cinnamon, nutmeg and eggs.

Gradually add flour. Dough will be sticky. Continue kneading with dough hook until smooth, about 5 minutes.

Cover bowl with plastic wrap and let the dough rest for 30-45 minutes.

After resting, knead until smooth and elastic, about 3 more minutes.

Add currants or raisins and knead until well mixed. Dough will still be sticky.

Shape dough into a ball, place in a buttered dish covered with plastic wrap and refrigerate overnight.

Let dough sit at room temperature for about ½ hour. Lightly grease a baking pan.

Divide dough into 24 equal pieces, place ½ inch apart on baking sheet, cover with towel, and let rise until double in size.

Preheat oven to 400 degrees.

When buns have risen, carefully slash buns with a cross pattern using a sharp or serrated knife. Brush buns with egg whites.

Bake for 10 minutes, then reduce the heat to 350 degrees. Bake until golden brown, about 15 minutes more. Remove to a wire rack.

Glaze Ingredients

- 1 1/3 c confectioners sugar
- 1 ½ tsp lemon zest
- ½ tsp lemon extract
- 1-2 TBS milk

Whisk together glaze ingredients; spoon over the buns in the cross pattern. Best if served warm.

Birthday Cake for Jesus

Whether it's homemade or store-bought, pastry or ice cream, don't miss the opportunity to share a birthday cake for Jesus each year. Perhaps you will want to giftwrap the family Bible and allow one child each year to unwrap God's wonderful gift of His Word. Even when your children get older, they will still look forward to this special family tradition!

Contact Us

Steve and Megan Scheibner travel extensively facilitating parenting, marriage, and men's and women's conferences for churches and other organizations.

Conferences Available Include:
- Parenting Matters
  Marriage Matters
  Character Matters
  Second Mile Leadership for Men
- When God Writes Your Story
  The Wise Wife
  The A-Z of a Character Healthy Homeschool
- The Discipling Mom
- and more....

To speak with Steve or Megan please call:

1-877-577-2736 or, send them an email by clicking the Contact Us tab at:

Characterhealth.com

also, follow them on twitter:
@SteveScheibner
@Meganscheibner
@CharacterHealth

Other Books by Megan Ann Scheibner:

In My Seat:
A Pilot's Story from Sept. 10th–11th

Grand Slam:
An Athletes Guide to Success in Life

Rise and Shine:
Routines and Recipes For Your Morning

Lunch and Literature

Dinner and Discipleship

Studies in Character

An A to Z Guide For Characterhealthy Homeschooling

Other Books by Steve Scheibner:
Bible Basics (Now available with a DVD for small group studies)

Books by Steve and Megan Scheibner:
Eight Rules of Communication For Successful Marriages

Studies in Character

The King of Thing and the Kingdom of Thingdom

DVD Series Available:

Parenting Matters:
The Nine Practices of the Pro-Active Parent

Character Matters:
The Nine Practices of Character Healthy Youth

The Toddler Toolbox

Battling With Behavior

Bible Basics

Subscribe to Steve and Megan's blogs:

- *www.SteveScheibner.com*
- *www.MeganScheibner.com*

You can find these books and other resources at:

www.characterhealth.com

BIOGRAPHY OF MEGAN SCHEIBNER

Megan was born March 13th 1962 and came home to her adoptive family March 15th. She grew up in York, PA and graduated from York Suburban H.S. in 1980. Four years later, she earned a B.A. in Speech Communications from West Chester University. She uses her degree as she teaches and speaks at conferences and women's ministry functions, as well as in individual and couples counseling.

Megan is the home schooling mother of eight beautiful children, four boys and four girls. She has been married for 29 years to her college sweetheart, Steve Scheibner. Together they have co-authored Parenting Matters, The Nine

Practices of the Pro-Active Parent. She is also the author of a series of discipleship books for mothers and several devotional Bible studies. She authored, "In My Seat," the story of Steve's 9/11 experience, that has captivated millions on YouTube. Her newest book, "An A-Z Guide For Character-Healthy Homeschooling" provides encouragement and practical tips gained through her 20 plus years of homeschooling experience. She is a popular speaker, guest on Family Talk with Dr. James Dobson, and TV personality on the Glenn Beck TV show.

Megan and her husband Steve share a strong desire to equip today's parents to raise the next generation of character healthy leaders. In her spare time, she loves to run and play tennis. Megan enjoys writing, cooking, feeding teenagers, reading, and everything pertaining to the Boston Red Sox.

Books by Megan:
- Character Matters: A Daily Step-By-Step Guide To Developing Courageous Character
- Eight Rules of Communication For Successful Marriages
- An A-Z Guide For Character-Healthy Homeschooling
- In My Seat: A Pilot's Story From Sept.10th-11th.
- Grand Slam: A Four Week Devotional Bible Study For Christian Athletes.
- Rise and Shine: Recipes and Routines For Your Morning.
- Lunch and Literature.
- Dinner and Discipleship.
- Studies in Character.
- The King of Thing and The Kingdom of Thingdom.

NOTES:

....
....
....
....
....
....
....
....
....
....
....
....
....
....
....

NOTES:

NOTES:

....

....

....

....

....

....

....

....

....

....

....

....

....

....

NOTES:

....

....

....

....

....

....

....

....

....

....

....

....

....

....

....

NOTES:

....

....

....

....

....

....

....

....

....

....

....

....

....

....

....

....

NOTES:

....
....
....
....
....
....
....
....
....
....
....
....
....
....
....
....
....

NOTES: